A DIOCESAN SERVICE BOOK

A DIOCESAN SERVICE BOOK

SERVICES AND PRAYERS
FOR
VARIOUS OCCASIONS

Edited and ordered by
LESLIE STANNARD HUNTER
Bishop of Sheffield 1939–1962

LONDON
OXFORD UNIVERSITY PRESS
NEW YORK   TORONTO
1965

Oxford University Press, Amen House, London E.C.4

GLASGOW NEW YORK TORONTO MELBOURNE WELLINGTON
BOMBAY CALCUTTA MADRAS KARACHI LAHORE DACCA
CAPE TOWN SALISBURY NAIROBI IBADAN ACCRA
KUALA LUMPUR HONG KONG

Printed in Great Britain by
W. & J. Mackay & Co. Ltd., Chatham

FOREWORD

I believe it is in worship that we men and women can discover our unities most clearly and sharply. All our separatenesses—cultures, words, traditions—can be brought together and offered in the great free acts of worship; and in the common offering we can discover one another, and the unities God has given us. I say 'can', because the discovery does not happen automatically. It comes only with the objectivity, the simplicity, and the greatness which are the hall-marks of true worship. But the discovery can be made.

The Anglican Communion is one company of Christians which has learned the full force of this. It is in our common worship that all our deepest brotherhood is found. The lesser intimations of unity have largely disappeared from Anglican life. The common cultural background, the pre-eminence of the English tongue, the tradition of the English Reformation settlement—none of these now is a cardinal bond of unity. More and more we find how profoundly the word 'Communion' describes our brotherhood, symbolic of precisely the truth that common worship is the locus of unity above all others.

And what is true of Anglicans is true of all Christians, and of wider associations still. It is in worship that we can discover the unity God has given us. Therefore when a book of worship such as this is given to us—acts of worship marked with objectivity, simplicity, greatness—our impulse rightly is to hope that Christians in every land and church may know it and use it, and so be helped toward mutual discovery and unity.

The prayers and offices it contains are for many different occasions. Some, no doubt, may be appropriate only in the Church of England. But most of them meet what are surely universal liturgical needs, bringing to those occasions forms of worship marked by precisely the wholeness of offering and receiving which Bishop Hunter describes so vividly in the Introduction.

They will meet many needs; and I hope they may find wide use in our Anglican family and outside it and so help many people to share one another's gifts and see more clearly the common gifts which make us one in Christ.

Ascension Day, 1963

STEPHEN F. BAYNE, JR.
Bishop
Executive Officer of the
Consultative Body of the Lambeth
Conference

CONCERNING THE WORSHIP OF THE CHURCH

Worship is not only a duty which man owes to God; it is, when sincere and corporate, a refreshment and a joy. Christian worship is not only an act of devotion in a church, it comprehends the whole of a man's life and is more perfectly an offering and service to God when that life is truly and responsibly a service to men. This it becomes when, humbly offered through the Lord Jesus Christ, it is impregnated with his thought and action Godward and manward.

Human nature and society being as far short of the Divine perfection and the Kingdom of God as they are, it often happens that the unity of worship and life is broken and the wholeness of the worshipful life becomes split up. In times of trouble, when the spirit of man is cramped and the life of the Church under duress, theology and piety have been tempted to make a sharp distinction between prayer and action, between the obligation of worship and man's secular obedience which is not in harmony with the Gospel. When this happens piety becomes an end in itself and escapist in temper, so that the people of God lose a Christian concern for the world and forget their apostleship.

The temptation of the godly has always been to think the devil was right when he claimed to have this world in his power. But this world is God's world and the universe as we now know it to be is his creative Word. Therefore Christians have not to think the worst of it, but thankfully to make the best of it. Their thought of God, to whom their prayers and adoration are directed, will not belittle either the grandeur of his creative activity in the universe or the wideness and depth of his mercy in his redemptive action of which the Bible is the record. Christian worship will always be finely stretching for us poor humans, but it should never become a tedious exercise. It only tends to become that when for one reason or another it does not grow out of man's life and work, and does not find its Amen and fulfilment in them.

The anxiety of those who value the Church's liturgy and the richness of our liturgical inheritance should be that so large a proportion of Western society today is not sharing in this inheritance and that many good people whose lives are not unworshipful find 'public worship dull and un-inspiring to the point of being distasteful'. Some church-men write this off by saying that the mental climate and the pressures of modern life—science, technology, the long fight of the workers for bread and social justice—have destroyed men's 'religious' faculties and their trust in Providence. That may be true up to a point, but it is not the whole truth. Scientist and technologist are not deprived by their studies of the worshipful attitude, neither are all non-church-goers pagans. For better or for worse people of all ages can no longer put up with being bored in church as patiently as previous generations apparently did; and certainly they are not blameworthy for being critical if what is done is carelessly done and falls below a standard of performance expected nowadays in comparable activites.

Even if it were true that modern man finds it more difficult to get on to his knees than medieval man did, then it would be the more important to try to ensure that in their normal Sunday worship congregations should be engaged in an act which is lively because it is integrated

with the life of the world and joyful because it is truly
directed to the Father of Jesus Christ and filled with the
Holy Spirit. Moreover, there is evidence from all parts of
the world that in churches where love, care, and intelli-
gence are put into the worship, Sunday by Sunday, people
on the fringe of our churches respond.

A printed order of service is like a play without the actors
and the producer. Even Shakespeare can be ruined by bad
acting and poor presentation. An order of service, be it
simple or elaborate, is only the bare bones which those
who have to make it actual, clergy and people together, can
sublimate or wreck. The ceremonial, especially when
simple, has to fit the particular building and ought to be
carefully rehearsed in that building. Unsuitable music, in-
appropriate hymns, lack of rhythm in processions, fussiness
of vergers and sidesmen, absence of silence, undue haste or
slowness, careless speech, bad reading of Scripture, ten-
minute sermons that are too long by ten minutes, will spoil
the finest of liturgies, and will wreck the more imperfect
and occasional uses set out in this book. Not taking trouble
is always dull and tedious alike in giving and receiving.
On the other hand, a congregation, a choir, and clergy will
find a delight in trying to make their acts of worship an
open channel of communication along which the Spirit of
God can travel.

There are five points in the Common Prayer of our
Communion to which special care and thought need con-
stantly to be given, both in normal Sunday worship and
in the occasional offices and special services.

I. PREPARATION FOR WORSHIP

What is done at the time and well done depends on
what is done before the time, and done quietly and in order.

No new church should be built with less than three

vestries, one for the officiating clergy, one for the lay
officers, and one for the choir. They should be of sufficient
size and adequately appointed with cupboards where
cassocks and surplices can be hung without being crushed
—each member of the choir having his allotted space.

To arrive in time and in the right temper and attitude
of mind is important for congregation as well as for clergy,
lay officers, and choir. So also is what happens at the west
end of the church and in the vestries. Garrulity accompanied by much hissing does not improve the occasion.
Everyone should know what each and all are going to do in
church. A little enforced silence is more likely to induce
the right attitude rather than an intoned collect or one
hastily said. The books on the clergy and choir stalls should
have been opened beforehand, and made ready for use.
Another contribution to good preparation is that the
members of the congregation should be induced to sit
together without being crowded, and at the front of the
nave near the clergy and not at the back, and that they
should be supplied with Prayer Book and hymn-book.
If the service is a special one then it should be clearly
explained to the congregation, including the lay officers,
before it starts. Even if it is a normal statutory service the
congregation should be told what the theme is and how the
psalms, hymns, and lessons are—if they are—related to it.

The entry (and outgoing) of the clergy and choir can
and should be a worshipful act. This will only happen if
they are rehearsed frequently, so that the pairs are evenly
spaced with at least a yard between them, and the speed of
walking is neither a very slow amble nor a disorganized
rush. It is not necessary to cover up the lack of drill by the
singing of a hymn. If there is a case for allowing a congregation to pull itself together before the liturgy begins
by singing a hymn this should not be confused with cover-

ing up the tramp of the choristers. And there is no case for adding a PS. to the final Blessing by yet another hymn and a loudly-sung vestry prayer.

The clergy and choir in their places, a short but complete silence should follow. If any should doubt the spiritual efficacy of this let him come to Taizé, where I happen to be writing, and feel the influence of the periods of sustained silence at the beginning and ending of the Office—and also during it. There is too little silence in our services: item follows item without pause—or moments of silence—like a paragraph of print in which the punctuation has been omitted.

Care with these details helps to ensure that the congregation not only attends but participates actively. Those of us who lead the worship of a congregation and the regular worshippers need to remind ourselves continually that every statutory service is a 'special' service for someone present at it. Every service therefore should have the care and attention to detail that we instinctively take on special occasions.

2. THE VALUE OF SILENCE

A non-conformist layman once complained: 'Anglican services are so restless—one is always having to stand up, sit, kneel, and is never allowed just to be still and reflect.' A fair criticism. There is so much to get through that the pauses are cut out. The minister gets to his feet and begins the *Gloria* while the congregation is still struggling to disengage from the hassocks: the reader of the Lesson arrives at the lectern before the psalm is ended and begins before the people are seated and so encourages non-attention: the sermon is no sooner ended than we plunge into a hymn and the business of a collection. At a Choral Eucharist even good organists seem to feel that all the

pauses or possible moments for reflection and private
prayer must be filled with sound. During the Administration they are tempted to doodle on the organ or to spatter
the period with verses of hymns sung at intervals, which
defeats both private prayer and intelligent hymn-singing.
The spiritual and liturgical loss from this insistence on
sound is great.

3. INTERCESSION

The chief periods of intercession in our Church's
Common Prayer are the Litany, the Prayer for the Church
Militant in the liturgy, and after the Third Collect in
Morning and Evening Prayer.

The Litany would be improved by a few minor alterations in its wording and two or three additional suffrages,
e.g. for unity in the Church, peace in the world, family life,
and the day's work. It would also aid the Church's intercession if its suffrages were rearranged in three groups that
could sometimes be used separately (cf. pp. 187-94).

It would be a great enrichment of the Church's worship
if the Liturgical Commission could compose an Act of
Praise and Thanksgiving, similar in pattern and comparable in quality with the Litany.

The Prayer for the Church would be more prayable by a
congregation if it were broken into sections and each
section ended with an 'Amen', or a brief response like
'Lord hear our prayer'. If that were done then the more
comprehensive, 1928, version would hold the co-operation
of the people better. There might also be a place allowed
in it for free particularized intercessions, fuller than a
bidding of a special intention. There is nothing to be said
for long, impromptu biddings before the prayer which
too often only say clumsily what the prayer expresses
succinctly and perfectly.

After the Third Collect, in place of the State prayers, more flexible and varied intercessions are now commonly used, and often taken with much care.

Because a number of prayers for special objects and occasions are included in this book, it is not intended to suggest that the best way to draw a congregation into intercession is a string of short prayers, even if each is preceded with 'Let us pray for . . .'. This is a temptation to which one easily yields if the preparation for the service is too hurried. A better way is a Litany with responses, of which there are now many available. Best of all is to tell the congregation before they kneel: 'We are going to intercede for . . ., and to offer thanksgiving for . . .', being careful to limit the number of each to three or four, and to add: 'I shall mention each subject in turn and leave a time for silent prayer after each.' Then when the people have knelt down and there is silence, preface the biddings with an introductory prayer (cf. p. 174) and conclude with a general prayer, like the 'prayer for all sorts and conditions of men', or maybe a shorter one; similarly, conclude the thanksgivings with the General Thanksgiving said together or a short Ascription or Doxology; and finally to end the exercise with silent prayer for ourselves summed up in St. Chrysostom's prayer or simply the Grace said corporately. If a variety of methods are used a congregation will become more flexible and co-operating; and the intercession will be a part of the Church's ministry to the world.

4. THE USE OF HYMNS

In our country as in Germany hymns are popular. They were, however, only mated to the Book of Common Prayer at the beginning of the nineteenth century. As one sometimes meets them by the handful in our Sunday services one feels that hymns and the liturgy are like two people living apart though under one roof. Hymns are just interpolated in order to make the services more palatable to popular taste. Often this is done with so little reference to the content of the liturgical services that the choice of hymns is left to the organist.

Until the beginning of this century, the Church of England was not well served with hymn-books, as to either words or music. The publication of the *English Hymnal* was the dawn of a new day. One valuable though unobtrusive thing which its editors did (it was afterwards elaborated in *Songs of Praise*) was to include an appendix in which appropriate hymns were suggested for each of the Sunday services throughout the year and the place in the service where the hymn should be sung was also indicated. This is how hymns should be married to the liturgy, thereby enriching its movement and making it more congregational.

The more fully the variable parts of a service can be integrated one with another so as to make the act of worship a realized and felt whole, the more inspiring will it be to those who share in it; and surely therefore the more pleasing to God to whose praise it is. A discriminating and imaginative choice of the hymns for the Sunday services should be a labour of love, week by week, for the priest whose responsibility it is—not of course without consultation with his musical colleague. For as every priest and organist discovers when he tries to get rid of a bad tune, hymn and tune are a unit. A good hymn can be marred by a bad tune, while a strong tune may carry a weak hymn. Music in a subtle and penetrating way expresses values which are spiritual, even moral. Those who are arguing that music in church should be popular at any price are underestimating the cost. They should read the good sense that was talked and practised half a century ago by Vaughan

Williams, the Shaws, and some of their contemporaries in advocating what they called 'good popular'—even Plato might teach them a thing or two. Von Hügel's timely caution to chaplains made revolutionary and even angry young men by their experiences in the Army and Navy during the First World War is true: 'It is impossible to confine any adequate statement of the richness of life within any formula Tommy can understand; and if we do not get him to feel that the richness is there, all round him and within him, we shall never have him, indeed it is not worth trying to have him. . . . There are things beyond Tommy, and the minute he wakes up to this primary fact, we shall have a sign that he is saved.' 'Milk for babes'; oh yes; but unless they are mentally deficient, babes grow up. It would be a dim prospect for the mission of the People of God if congregations of adults were fed from pulpit and organ with baby food. Liveliness is as desirable in the worship of God as in the dance-hall, but it is another quality of liveliness. Both experiences may take a young person out of himself or herself but not by the same exit. One will lift him into God's free air and set him on the open road; the other may only lead into another room full of crowded humanity.

If hymns are to be used intelligently and integrated into the movement of the liturgy so as to make it the more moving, then sometimes only one or two verses of a hymn may serve the purpose. In the Church of England we are too fearful of singing only a part of a hymn, as the Scottish Church habitually does with its paraphrases and metrical psalms. Moreover, quite apart from the liturgical reason for using only some verses of a hymn at a particular place, the fact remains that many hymns have one or more feeble verses, because the poetical and spiritual inspiration of the writer falters. Let us be more flexible in our use of

hymnody, and so make people think about what they are
offering to God instead of being content with the relaxation
of a good sing as a sort of entr'acte.

It is because one cares so much to hear hymns well used
to enliven congregational worship and to give it colour and
enrichment, that in some of the services in this book hymns
have been printed in full and in other places an appropriate
choice of hymn has been suggested.*

5. THE PSALTER

What are we to do about the psalms in Sunday worship?
Is the only way to make their recital congregational to *say*
them antiphonally, not priest and people, but the two sides
of the church alternately, both joining in the *Glorias*? Can
the psalms be translated and set to music which is easy
to pick up and sing with a rhythm, as Père Gélineau S.J.
has done with such notable success in France using the
translation in *La Bible de Jérusalem*? English, especially
Coverdale's English, does not correspond to the rhythm of
Hebrew poetry and fit the 'Gélineau' rhythm so easily as
the French does.

The time is due, indeed overdue, for our Church to deal
drastically with the psalms in its Sunday worship. There
are some psalms which are unsuited to Sunday worship
because they are long or tedious or too consistently sub-
Christian. There are many others which contain obscure,
even meaningless verses because the text is corrupt, and
other verses which are unchristian. Our Church ought to
have the courage to be as ruthless in excisions as the French
Church is being, for we want the best of the psalms to
continue to be a deeply-rooted part of public worship,

---

* For each hymn, whether printed in full or indicated by first line,
some convenient sources for words and music are given in the Index,
pp. 198ff.

since they are more durable and satisfying than all but a few hymns.

An ordinary congregation of lay people will only read the words in their plain and obvious sense. They cannot be expected to read into them the subtle and mystical interpretations hallowed by monastic tradition, which is more possible within limits for those who say them in their daily offices. It is not desirable that they should be asked to try. It is of major importance that whether alone or in company we should mean what we sing and believe what we say when we speak to God. This sincerity is not incompatible with a humble recognition on the part of a worshipper, that his thoughts are far short of God's truth and that the worship of the Church on earth must often take him out of himself and beyond where he is.

In the Christian liturgy men and women are drawn into a two-way movement of man to God and God to man in the fellowship of the Holy Spirit. He takes us up the heavenly ladder and leads us back into our place and to our responsibility in the life of the world; and the beginning and ending are through and in Jesus Christ.

CONTENTS

FOREWORD BY BISHOP STEPHEN BAYNE v
PREFACE: CONCERNING THE WORSHIP OF THE
   CHURCH vii

I SERVICES FOR REGULAR DIOCESAN
   AND PAROCHIAL OCCASIONS
   The Laying of a Foundation Stone 1
   The Consecration of a Church and Dedication of
     Church Buildings 7
   The Consecration of a Burial Ground 16
   The Institution and Induction of an Incumbent 19
   The Commissioning of a Suffragan or Assistant
     Bishop 30
   The Collation and Installation of a Canon (or Arch-
     deacon) 34
   The Admission of a Chancellor 39
   The Commissioning and Licensing of a Deaconess
     or Woman Worker 45
   The Admission and Licensing of a Reader 50

II MEMORIALS AND DEDICATIONS
   A Memorial of a Churchman 56
   A Lady Chapel 57
   A Holy Table 59
   A Cross and Candlesticks 60
   A Rood 60
   A Bible or Lectern 62
   An Organ 63
   A Peal of Bells 65
   An Installation of Lighting 67
   A Chapel of Youth 68
   The Hallowing of a Dwelling or Conference House 71
   A Hospital Unit 74
   A School 75
   A General Prayer of Dedication 76

III OCCASIONAL OFFICES
   A Thanksgiving of Parents for the Birth of a Child 77
   The Public Baptism of Infants 80
     The revised order and directions approved by the
     Convocation of York, with some amendments after
     experimental use

Confirmation   89
     Introductory Note: Instructions to Clergy:
     Thoughts and Prayers: Hymns
A Form for Private Confession and Absolution   101
The Ministry to the Sick   103
     Introductory Note: Preparation: Laying on of
     Hands: Holy Communion: Anointing with Oil:
     Other Prayers and Commendations.
The Burial of the Dead   110
     An alternative service for public cemeteries and
     crematoria.
An Outline of a Memorial Service   118
The Depositing of Ashes   121

IV SPECIAL OCCASIONS
A Devotion on a Diocesan Occasion   124
Act of Dedication for a Newly Elected Parish Church
     Council or a Diocesan Council   128
A Diocesan Festival Service   130
A Service of Praise for Choirboys or Young People   137
A Family Service on Christmas Eve   142
A Carol Service during the Christmas Season or at
     Epiphany   145
Procession and Eucharist on Palm Sunday   152
Devotions for the Evenings in Holy Week before
     Good Friday   157
Festal Openings for Mattins and Evensong   on
     Ascension Day, Whitsunday, and Harvest   164
An Opening for a Civic Service and a Lesson or
     Lessons at the Same   168
Vestry Prayers   171

V PRAYERS FOR CHURCH AND SOCIETY
(A) Prayers
 1 Preparation for Intercession   174
 2 For a Mission of Teaching   174
 3 For the Mission of the Church   175
 4 Thanksgiving for a Missionary   176
 5 Commemorations of Four Servants of God: 176
          St. Francis   October 4
          St. Martin   November 11
          St. Hugh of Lincoln   November 17
          William Temple   (b. October 15)
 6 The Ecumenical Movement and Reunion. The Church
     Overseas   178

7   Prayers for a Diocese   178
        For Choirboys: for a Church under Repair.
8   For a Town   180
9   For the Health Services and Hospitals   180
10 For Social Services   181
11 For the Professions   181
12 For Home and Family Life   182
13 For Relatives and Friends   183
14 For Captives and Refugees   183
15 For Strangers and Immigrants   183
16 For Peace at Home and in the World   184
17 For an Industrial Area   184
18 For Industry and Commerce   185
19 For Agriculture   186
20 For Workers: Intercession   186
                    Thanksgiving   186
(B) The Suffrages in the Litany Arranged
        as Intercessions:

        (1) Opening Supplications   187
        (2) For the Life of the Church,   189
        (3) For the Life of the Nation and the World   191

EDITORIAL NOTE AND A DEDICATION   195
ACKNOWLEDGEMENTS   197
FIRST LINES OF HYMNS   198
    With recommended tunes, and sources

I

SERVICES FOR REGULAR DIOCESAN AND PAROCHIAL OCCASIONS

THE LAYING OF A FOUNDATION STONE OF A CHURCH*

THE PREPARATION

When all are assembled on the site there shall be sung:

> All people that on earth do dwell,
> Sing to the Lord with cheerful voice,
> Him serve with mirth, his praise forth tell,
> Come ye before him and rejoice.
>
> Know that the Lord is God indeed;
> Without our aid he did us make;
> We are his folk, he doth us feed;
> And for his sheep he doth us take.
>
> O enter then his gates with praise,
> Approach with joy his courts unto;
> Praise, laud, and bless his name always,
> For it is seemly so to do.
>
> For why? the Lord our God is good:
> His mercy is for ever sure;
> His truth at all times firmly stood,
> And shall from age to age endure.

* If the ceremony is in the open, how much of this Order can be used will depend on the time of year and the weather.

Then shall the priest of the parish say:

In the Name of God the Father, who has mercy upon all men; of God the Son, who died that we might live; and of God the Holy Spirit, who gives to men skill and wisdom, courage and love.

People: Amen.

V. Thy Kingdom, O Lord, is an everlasting kingdom;

R. And thy dominion endureth throughout all ages.

V. One generation shall praise thy works unto another;

R. And thy saints shall give thanks unto thee.

V. Praise ye the Lord;

R. The Lord's Name be praised.

Then shall be said, verse by verse, the eighty-fourth Psalm:

O how amiable are thy dwellings: thou Lord of hosts!

My soul hath a desire and longing to enter into the courts of the Lord: my heart and my flesh rejoice in the living God.

Yea, the sparrow hath found her an house, and the swallow a nest where she may lay her young: even thy altars, O Lord of hosts, my King and my God.

Blessed are they that dwell in thy house: they will be alway praising thee.

Blessed is the man whose strength is in thee: in whose heart are thy ways.

Who going through the vale of misery use it for a well: and the pools are filled with water.

They will go from strength to strength: and unto the God of gods appeareth every one of them in Sion.

O Lord God of hosts, hear my prayer: hearken, O God of Jacob.

Behold, O God our defender: and look upon the face of thine Anointed.

For one day in thy courts: is better than a thousand.

I had rather be a door-keeper in the house of my God: than to dwell in the tents of ungodliness.

For the Lord God is a light and defence: the Lord will give grace and worship, and no good thing shall he withhold from them that live a godly life.

O Lord God of hosts: blessed is the man that putteth his trust in thee.

Glory be to the Father . . .

THE THREE LESSONS

Hear the words of our Saviour Christ:

I am the Way, the Truth and the Life; no one comes to the Father but by me.

Greater love has no man than this, that a man lay down his life for his friends. You are my friends if you do the things which I command you.

You have not chosen me but I have chosen you and appointed you, that you should go and bring forth fruit.

Hear also the words of St. Paul:

Other foundation can no man lay than that is laid, which is Jesus Christ.

Who humbled himself, becoming obedient unto death, even the death of the Cross.

Wherefore God has highly exalted him and given him the name which is above every name; that at the name of Jesus every knee should bow, and that every tongue should confess that Jesus Christ is Lord to the glory of God the Father.

Now therefore you are fellow citizens with the saints and of the household of God: and are built upon the foundation of the apostles and prophets, Jesus Christ himself being the head corner-stone; in whom all the building fitly framed together grows into a holy temple in the Lord.

Hear also from the Revelation of St. John the Divine:

I heard a voice of many angels round about the throne, saying with a great voice: Worthy is the Lamb which was slain to receive power and riches and might and honour and glory and blessing.

And every created thing which is in heaven, and on the earth and under the earth heard I saying: Unto him that sitteth upon the throne and unto the Lamb, be the blessing and the honour and the glory and the dominion, for ever and ever. And the living creatures answered, Amen.

Then may be sung the hymn:

> Pray that Jerusalem may have
>   Peace and felicity:
> Let them that love thee and thy peace
>   Have still prosperity.
>
> Therefore I wish that peace may still
>   Within thy walls remain,
> And ever may thy palaces
>   Prosperity retain.
>
> Now, for my friends' and brethren's sake,
>   Peace be in thee, I'll say,
> And for the house of God our Lord
>   I'll seek thy good alway.

THE PRAYERS

Thereafter the Bishop shall bid the people to prayer, saying:

> The Lord be with you;

Answer: And with thy Spirit.

> Let us pray.

Almighty and Eternal God, Lord of heaven and earth, who art present to thy children when they call upon thee: Hallow this place where we now lay the foundations of a House to the praise and worship of thy Name, and grant that thy servants may see the fruition of their work; through Jesus Christ our Lord. *Amen.*

And laying his hand upon the Stone he shall proceed:

O Lord Jesus Christ, Son of the living God, the brightness of the Father's glory and the express image of his Person, the rock of our strength and of our salvation; Bless the laying of this Stone in thy name, and be thou, we beseech thee, the beginning, the increase, and the consummation of this our work, who with the Father and the Holy Spirit livest and reignest one God, world without end. *Amen.*

Then, all things being made ready, the Stone shall be laid by the person appointed with these words:

In the faith of Jesus Christ, we place this Stone; in the Name of God the Father, the Son, and the Holy Spirit. *Amen.*

After silence has been kept for a space all shall join together in saying:

Our Father . . . for ever and ever. Amen.

And the Bishop shall continue:

Unto him that is able to keep us from falling;

Unto him that is able by the word of his grace to build us up;

Unto him that is able to do exceeding abundantly above all that we ask or think according to the power that worketh in us;

Unto him be glory in the Church by Jesus Christ throughout all ages, world without end.

And all shall respond:

> O friends, in gladness let us sing,
> Supernal anthems echoing,
>   Alleluia, Alleluia!
> To God the Father, God the Son,
> And God the Spirit, Three in One.
>   Alleluia!

Thereafter the Archdeacon or some other priest shall say:

V. Except the Lord build the house;

R. They labour but in vain that build it.

O God, without whom nothing is strong and nothing is holy: help thy servants, we beseech thee, to accomplish this work, and by thy inspiration to make it beautiful and good. Bless those who are its donors and prosper their service to thy glory: protect and guide all the builders; prepare the hearts and minds of those who will minister and worship here in days to come: to the hallowing of thy Name and the proclaiming of thy Kingdom through Jesus Christ our Lord. *Amen.*

O Almighty God, who hast built thy Church upon the foundation of the Apostles and Prophets, Jesus Christ himself being the chief corner-stone; Grant us so to be joined together in unity of spirit by their doctrine, that we may be made an holy temple acceptable unto thee; through Jesus Christ our Lord. *Amen.*

Prevent us, O Lord, in all our doings with thy most gracious favour, and further us with thy continual help; that in all our works, begun, continued, and ended in thee, we may glorify thy holy Name, and finally by thy mercy obtain everlasting life; through Jesus Christ our Lord. *Amen.*

HYMN, *followed by* THE BLESSING

THE CONSECRATION OF A CHURCH AND DEDICATION OF CHURCH BUILDINGS

The Church is to be furnished before the day of the Consecration in accordance with the use of the Church of England and the instructions of the Ordinary. The Archdeacon or other person duly appointed shall inspect the Church and report whether such instructions have been observed.

THE PREPARATION

Where the plan of the building and the weather allow, it is customary for the Bishop in procession to make a circuit of the church before approaching the main entrance. As the procession approaches the door he shall say,

> The Lord be with you;
> *R.* And with thy spirit.

And all shall continue with him,

> Lord, have mercy upon us.
> Christ, have mercy upon us.
> Lord, have mercy upon us.

Our Father . . .

Meanwhile the congregation within shall sing a hymn, and then shall turn to face the door in silence until the Bishop's knock is heard.

THE ENTRY

The Bishop shall knock with his staff three times upon the door which is fast, saying,

Lift up your heads, O ye gates, and be ye lift up ye everlasting doors; And the King of glory shall come in.

From within the churchwardens shall say,

Who is the King of glory?

And the Bishop shall answer,

The Lord of hosts, he is the King of glory.

Then the Churchwardens, having opened the door, shall present to him a petition for the Consecration (or Dedication) with the keys of the building, saying,

Reverend Father in God, we pray you to dedicate, consecrate, and bless this Church.

The Bishop's procession having passed through the doors, he shall say,

Peace be to this house from God our heavenly Father,

Answer: Amen.

Bishop: Peace be to this house from his Son who is our Peace,

Answer: Amen.

Bishop: Peace be to this house from the Holy Spirit the Comforter.

Answer: Amen.

Bishop: Glory be to the Father and to the Son and to the Holy Ghost:

People: As it was in the beginning, is now, and ever shall be. Amen.

All shall turn towards the Sanctuary and the Bishop shall say a Prayer of Dedication,

Almighty and ever-living God, from whom cometh every good and perfect gift, be pleased to accept the gifts and labours of many people which have enabled us to complete and furnish *these buildings*. Use *them*, we beseech thee, for thy purposes and hallow *them* with thy blessing. May thy Holy Spirit refresh and quicken those who come here and as our Lord hath promised lead them into all truth with all charity: so that by them thy mercy and love may radiate into the homes and lives of the people of this neighbourhood; to the glory of Jesus Christ our Lord. *Amen.*

Then, as the Bishop moves into the Sanctuary, Psalm 122 shall be sung.

THE SEPARATION OF THE CHURCH FROM ALL UNHALLOWED USES

All kneeling, a priest shall say or sing a portion of the Litany while the Bishop alone, carrying his staff, shall measure the Church from East to West and from North to South and trace a St. Andrew's Cross on the floor at the entrance to the Chancel or Sanctuary, thus representing the joining of the four corners of the Church and marking it with Christ's Name for ever. (X is the first letter of Christ's Name in the Greek.)

O holy, blessed, and glorious Trinity, three Persons and one God:

Have mercy upon us miserable sinners.

Remember not, Lord, our offences, nor the offences of our forefathers; neither take thou vengeance of our sins: spare us, good Lord, spare thy people, whom thou hast redeemed with thy most precious blood, and be not angry with us for ever.

Spare us, good Lord.

From all blindness of heart; from pride, vain-glory, and hypocrisy; from envy, hatred, and malice, and all uncharitableness,

Good Lord, deliver us.

By the mystery of thy holy Incarnation; by thy holy Nativity and Circumcision; by thy Baptism, Fasting, and Temptation,

Good Lord, deliver us.

By thine Agony and bloody Sweat; by thy Cross and Passion; by thy precious Death and Burial; by thy glorious Resurrection and Ascension; and by the coming of the Holy Ghost,

Good Lord, deliver us.

In all time of our tribulation; in all time of our wealth; in the hour of death, and in the day of judgement,

Good Lord, deliver us.

We sinners do beseech thee to hear us, O Lord God: and that it may please thee to rule and govern thy holy Church universal in the right way;

We beseech thee to hear us, good Lord.

That it may please thee to keep and strengthen in the true worshipping of thee, in righteousnes and holiness of life, thy Servant Elizabeth, our most gracious Queen and Governor;

We beseech thee to hear us, good Lord.

That it may please thee to illuminate all Bishops, Priests, and Deacons, with true knowledge and understanding of thy Word: and that both by their preaching and living they may set it forth and show it accordingly;

We beseech thee to hear us, good Lord.

That it may please thee to further the work of thy Church in all the world, and to send forth labourers into the harvest;

We beseech thee to hear us, good Lord.

That it may please thee to bless and keep all thy people;

We beseech thee to hear us, good Lord.

That it may please thee to give us an heart to love and dread thee, and diligently to live after thy commandments;

We beseech thee to hear us, good Lord.

That it may please thee to give to all thy people increase of grace to hear meekly thy Word, and to receive it with pure affection, and to bring forth the fruits of the Spirit;

We beseech thee to hear us, good Lord.

That it may please thee to bring into the way of truth all such as have erred, and are deceived;

We beseech thee to hear us, good Lord.

That it may please thee to strengthen such as do stand: and to comfort and help the weak-hearted; and to raise up them that fall; and finally to beat down Satan under our feet;

We beseech thee to hear us, good Lord.

That it may please thee to have mercy upon all men;

We beseech thee to hear us, good Lord.

That it may please thee to give us true repentance; to forgive us all our sins, negligences, and ignorances; and to endue us with the grace of thy Holy Spirit to amend our lives according to thy holy Word;

We beseech thee to hear us, good Lord.

And the Bishop, standing in the Sanctuary, shall continue,

Eternal God, whom eye hath not seen nor ear heard and whose praises no man can utter, whom the heavens cannot contain, much less buildings made with hands; vouchsafe, O Lord, to be present with us who are gathered here with humility and readiness of heart to consecrate this Church to the honour of thy Name. We desire to dedicate it entirely to thy service: for the reading of thy Word and the preaching of thy Gospel: for celebrating thy holy Sacraments, and offering to thee the sacrifices of prayer and thanksgiving. Accept, O Lord, this service at our hands, and bless it with such success as may hasten thy Kingdom and the salvation of thy children: through Jesus Christ our Lord. *Amen.*

LESSON

Jeremiah 9. 23–24, followed by 1 Peter 2. 1–9, or as the consecrating Bishop and Preacher may choose.

HYMN

THE CONSECRATION

All kneel and, after silence has been kept for a space, the Bishop, standing before the Holy Table, shall proceed,

The Lord be with you;
R. And with thy Spirit.

Lift up your hearts;
R. We lift them up unto the Lord.

Let us give thanks unto our Lord God;
R. It is meet and right so to do.

It is very meet, right, and our bounden duty, that we should at all times, and in all places, give thanks unto thee,

O Lord, Holy Father, Almighty, Everlasting God, who hast promised by Jesus our Lord to be present in the prayers and holy rites and faithful service of thy servants who call upon thee.

Hear us, O blessed and merciful Father, eternal in Love and Power: O Christ, our Saviour, entering into thy glory by the Cross, to whom all authority is given: O Holy Spirit, quickening and renewing all thought and life: O Holy and glorious Trinity blessed for evermore:

And vouchsafe to consecrate and continue thy blessing upon this Church in honour of . . . and to hallow this Holy Table for the perpetual Memorial of the perfect Sacrifice once offered upon the Cross: and grant that the prayers of those who worship here may be fulfilled according to thy will, their lives enriched by thy manifold grace, and their fellowship in the service of thy Kingdom strengthened and confirmed.

And unto thee, O God most holy, whose gifts are beyond count or measure or price, be the praise and the glory, world without end. *Amen.*

Then all shall say with the Bishop:

Our Father . . .

And, standing up, shall sing:

> Praise God from whom all blessings flow;
> Praise him all creatures here below;
> Praise him above, ye heavenly host;
> Praise Father, Son, and Holy Ghost.

THE WITNESS OF CONSECRATION ON STONE AND ON PARCHMENT

The Bishop shall mark the Cross of Consecration upon the Stone; which done, he shall say:

D.S.B.–C

This dwelling is God's habitation: it is a possession above all price which may not be spoken against.

Then shall the Bishop be seated in a chair before the Altar and, a table having been placed before him, he shall order the Sentence of Consecration to be read, saying:

Let the congregation be seated and let the Sentence of Consecration be read.

After the reading the Bishop shall sign the Sentence, others witnessing the deed by their signatures. When this has been done the congregation shall stand and the Bishop shall make

THE PROCLAMATION

By virtue of our sacred office in the Church of God, we do now declare to be consecrated and set apart from all common and secular uses this Church (*or* the portion of this building set apart to be the Church) of . . .

In the Name of God, Father, Son, and Holy Ghost. *Amen.*

HYMN

THE SERMON

A THANK-OFFERING

(*during which an anthem may be sung*)

HYMN *or* TE DEUM

Then all shall kneel, and shall say with the Bishop:

O God and Father of all, whom the whole heavens adore; Let the whole earth also worship thee, all kingdoms obey thee, all tongues confess and praise thee, and the sons of men love thee and serve thee in peace, through Jesus Christ our Lord. Amen.

THE BLESSING

Note:

THE DEDICATIONS

If there be a chapel or any ornaments or furnishings given as memorials, the Bishop, moving to a convenient place, shall say one or more of the prayers following, immediately before the Consecration.

O worship the Lord in the beauty of holiness;

Answer: And let the whole earth stand in awe of him.

Almighty Father, Lord of heaven and earth, be pleased to accept these gifts of thy children for the service of this House of Prayer. All things come of thee and of thine own do we give thee. And grant that what art and costliness cannot make worthy of thy service may be hallowed by thy blessing; through Jesus Christ our Lord. *Amen.*

In the faith of Jesus our Lord we dedicate . . . to the memory of . . . In the name of God, Father, Son, and Holy Spirit. *Amen.*

O God, before whose face the generations rise and pass away, the strength of those who labour and the repose of the holy and blessed dead; We remember all who have faithfully lived and died, especially . . . Lift us into light and love, and give us at last our portion with those who have trusted in thee and striven to do thy will; And unto thy Name with the Church on earth and the Church in heaven, we ascribe honour and glory, world without end. *Amen.*

If there are halls and rooms attached, as in a dual-purpose building, they may be dedicated with these words,

In the faith of Jesus Christ and for the benefit of all God's people we dedicate these . . . to the praise of the Father, the Son, and the Holy Spirit. *Amen.*

(*Appropriate Hymns:*

For the Preparation:

All things are thine: no gift have we . . .
Jesus, where'er thy people meet . . .

After the Entry, as alternative to Psalm 122:

All people that on earth do dwell . . .
(*without doxology*)

During Dedications:

The Church of God a kingdom is . . .
(*with a break after v. 3 for dedicatory prayer*)

Or if no dedications:

Happy are they, they that love God . . .

Before the Sermon:

Christ is our corner-stone . . .

After the thank-offering:

Ye servants of God, your Master proclaim . . .
Praise to the Lord, the Almighty, the King of
creation . . .
Now thank we all our God . . .)

THE CONSECRATION OF A BURIAL GROUND

OR OF A NEW PORTION OF AN EXISTING ONE

The Deed of Conveyance or Donation of the Ground with such other documents as are requisite shall be laid before the Registrar and Legal Secretary to the Bishop, and approved before the day for the ceremony is fixed.

The boundary must be clearly marked, and in the case of a new Burial Ground enclosed, and the ground prepared for use before the appointed day.

On the day, if the weather is fine, a table and a chair should be placed at a convenient place on the boundary, and the people assembled there, unless it be arranged to begin the service in church.

At the time the Bishop shall be received at the entrance by the Incumbent, Churchwardens, and members of the P.C.C.: and in the case of a Public Cemetery by the Chairman and members of the controlling Board.

Although the traditional part of the ceremony is the procession round the bounds, it is better for this to be omitted in wet or stormy weather and, where possible, for the service to be held in the church or chapel. And in the case of a churchyard adjacent to a church, the procession might start from the church following a hymn, and the concluding prayers be said in church.

The Bishop shall say:

In the Name of God, Father, Son, and Holy Spirit, Amen.

The Lord be with you:
Answer: And with thy spirit.

Lord have mercy upon us:
Answer: Christ have mercy upon us:
Lord have mercy upon us.

Let us go forth in peace
Answer: In the name of the Lord.

Then shall the Bishop, preceded by the groundsmen (walking beside the Crucifer), and followed by the Registrar, the Clergy, choir, and lay people, process round the boundary of the ground to be consecrated, saying one or more of the following Psalms: 130, 90, 103, 23.

Thereafter those responsible shall present to the Bishop the Petition for Consecration, saying:

Reverend Father in God, we request you to consecrate this ground for the burial of our people.

The Bishop shall signify his assent, and sitting down shall bid the Registrar read the Sentence of Consecration, and after it has been read he shall sign it.

This done he shall stand and say:

By virtue of our authority in the Church of God we do now consecrate and set apart from all profane and common uses this Ground to be a resting-place for the bodies of those who have departed in the Lord: in the Name of the Father, the Son and the Holy Spirit. *Amen.*

The Blessing of the Eternal God be upon this place to sanctify it and keep it hallowed and holy from henceforth until the day of the Lord Jesus. *Amen.*

And all shall join with him in saying:

Our Father . . . and ever and ever. Amen.

Thereafter the Bishop may speak to those assembled of the significance of what has been done and of the proper care of a Burial Ground and of the graves within it.

HYMN

Then the Bishop shall say one or more of the following prayers and dismiss the people with a Blessing.

O God, the Protector of all that trust in thee, without whom nothing is strong, nothing is holy; Increase and multiply upon us thy mercy; that thou being our ruler and guide, we may so pass through things temporal, that we finally lose not the things eternal: Grant this, O heavenly Father, for Jesus Christ's sake, our Lord. *Amen.*

The Collects for Easter Eve and Easter IV.

BLESSING

THE INSTITUTION AND INDUCTION
OF AN INCUMBENT

NOTE

The Ceremony has two parts: the legal preliminaries, and the act of worship. (It is called a Collation when the Bishop is the patron.)

The legal preliminaries, both those prior to and during the service, are designed to ensure, as far as may be, that the Clerk to be instituted has been chosen with care and with due attention to the needs and character of the parish and that he is a good Christian man, loyal to the tenets of the Church of England, obedient to its discipline, and dutiful to the Queen's Majesty.

In the Act of Worship the Incumbent is instituted by the Bishop of the diocese or by his deputy. The new Incumbent and the people of the parish, having been reminded of the duties and joys of their corporate witness and service in Christ Jesus our Lord, offer themselves to God and receive his commission and blessing.

The fashion whereby the people of the parish are ousted from their seats in the Church by a large influx from the parish the Incumbent has left robs the service of its significance. Similarly, the social hour which usually follows should be an occasion for the new Incumbent (and his wife) to meet one by one the members of his new congregation and other parishioners including ministers and members of other Christian congregations in the parish.

A Chair shall be set for the Bishop at the entrance to the Chancel. The Incumbent-designate and the Patron shall sit at the front of the seats in the Nave, and when the legal preliminaries take place in Church, a small table upon which shall be a copy of the New Testament, a pen, ink, and blotting paper shall be set below the Chancel step to the Bishop's right.

THE LEGAL PRELIMINARIES

These may take place either in the Vestry, if it is commodious, in the presence of the Churchwardens, representatives of the P.C.C., the Patron, and the Archdeacon or Rural Dean or their deputies, or they may be held in the Church at the entrance to the Chancel, but in this case the Declaration against Simony is more conveniently made previously in the Vestry.

The Bishop having seated himself, the Patron or his representative shall present the Clerk to him, saying:

Reverend Father in God, I present unto you this meet and proper person to be admitted to the cure of souls in this parish.

Then shall the Bishop say:

Whereas *A.B.*, Clerk, has been duly nominated for this office, his name publicly made known and no objection alleged, and his character and conduct properly commended to us, it is our good will to admit him to this cure; wherefore let the Declarations be made and subscribed and the Oaths taken according to law.

The Clerk shall then make the Declarations and shall subscribe his name thereto.

I. The Declaration of Assent

I, *A.B.*, Clerk, about to be admitted (and instituted) to the Vicarage (or Rectory or Perpetual Curacy) of . . . in the . . . and Diocese of . . . do solemnly make the following Declaration:

I assent to the Thirty-nine Articles of Religion and to the Book of Common Prayer, and of the Ordering of Bishops, Priests, and Deacons. I believe the Doctrine of the Church of England, as therein set forth, to be agreeable to the Word of God; and in Public Prayer and Administration of the Sacraments I will use the form in the said Book prescribed and none other, except so far as shall be ordered by lawful Authority.

II. The Declaration against Simony

[This long Declaration says in effect that neither the Incumbent, nor anybody else on his behalf, has secured the Presentation by corrupt means. Neither has he given any promise or entered into any covenant to resign at any time.]

After which, holding the New Testament in his right hand, he shall take the Oaths and sign his name to the documents.

I. The Oath of Allegiance

I, *A.B.*, Clerk, swear by Almighty God that I will be faithful and bear true Allegiance to Her Majesty Queen Elizabeth II, her heirs and successors according to law. So help me God.

II. The Oath of Canonical Obedience

I, *A.B.*, Clerk, swear by Almighty God that I will render true and Canonical Obedience to the Lord Bishop of . . . and his successors, in all things lawful and honest. So help me God.

Then, if the ceremony has taken place in the Church, the opening hymn shall be announced, and all stand.

THE ORDER OF SERVICE

When the Bishop, Incumbent-designate, Clergy, and Choir have entered and have proceeded to their respective places, a hymn of worship and adoration shall be sung, such as

Immortal, invisible, God only wise . . .

The Hymn ended, the Bishop shall say,

May God in all things be glorified through Jesus Christ to whom be worship and praise.

People: Evermore. Amen.

Bishop: Whosoever shall confess that Jesus is the Son of God, God abideth in him and he in God. Beloved, if God so loved us, we ought to love one another.

People: Amen.

Bishop: It is the will of God that all men should be saved and come to the knowledge of the truth.

People: Thanks be to thee, O God.

Bishop: Good people, forasmuch therefore as the care of immortal souls, for whom Christ died, and the charge and ordering of a church are so weighty and solemn a trust, we beseech you to join with us in prayer to Almighty God, our heavenly Father, that he would give to his servant, now called to the cure of souls in this parish, the manifold riches of his grace.

[*All kneel*]

Silence shall be kept that prayer may be made unto God, and thereafter the Bishop shall say:

> Lord have mercy upon us.
> *R.* Christ have mercy upon us.
> Lord have mercy upon us.

Grant, O Lord, to thy faithful people pardon and peace, that they may be cleansed from all their sins and serve thee with a quiet mind; through Jesus Christ our Lord. *Amen.*

Remember, O Lord, what thou hast wrought for us and not what we deserve, and as thou hast called us to thy service make us worthy of our calling; through Jesus Christ our Lord. *Amen.*

> *V.* Blessed are they that dwell in thy house;
> *R.* They will alway be praising thee.

O Almighty God, who hast built thy Church upon the foundation of the Apostles and Prophets, Jesus Christ himself being the head corner-stone; grant us so to be joined together in unity of spirit by their doctrine that we may be made an holy temple acceptable unto thee; through Jesus Christ our Lord. *Amen.*

V. Blessed is the man whose strength is in thee;

R. And in whose heart are thy ways.

Almighty God, the giver of all good gifts, who of thy divine providence hast appointed divers orders in thy Church: give thy grace, we humbly beseech thee, to all those who are called to any office or administration in the same, and especially to this thy servant, *A.B.*, now present before thee; and so replenish him with the truth of thy doctrine and endue him with innocency of life, that he may faithfully serve before thee, to the glory of thy great Name and the benefit of thy holy Church; through Jesus Christ our Lord. *Amen.*

[Thereafter may be sung, all still kneeling, the hymn,

Come, Holy Ghost, our souls inspire.]

[All stand]

Then the Bishop, sitting in his chair, shall read the Deed of Institution, the Clerk to be instituted kneeling before him and holding the seal thereof in his hands.

After which, the Bishop shall deliver the Deed to him, saying:

Receive your cure my care. In the Name of the Father, the Son, and the Holy Spirit. Amen.

Then shall be sung Psalm 122, 1–3, 5–9.

I was glad when they said unto me:
> We will go into the house of the Lord.

Our feet shall stand in thy gates:
> O Jerusalem.

Jerusalem is built as a city:
> That is at unity in itself. . . .

For there is the seat of judgement:
> Even the seat of the House of David.

O pray for the peace of Jerusalem:
> They shall prosper that love thee.

Peace be within thy walls:
> And plenteousness within thy palaces.

For my brethren and companions' sakes:
> I will wish thee prosperity.

Yea, because of the house of the Lord our God:
> I will seek to do thee good.

Glory be to the Father . . .

or, if there be no choir, the Hymn,

The Church of God a Kingdom is.

THE INDUCTION

If there be an Induction, the Bishop shall give the mandate to the Archdeacon (or his deputy) before the Psalm is begun, and thereupon the Archdeacon shall, with the Churchwardens and the Incumbent, proceed during the singing to the door of the Church, the Bishop meanwhile going to the Font and the Congregation turning accordingly. The Archdeacon, passing out, shall lay the hand of the Incumbent upon the handle of the door and shall say:

By virtue of this mandate I do induct you into the real, actual, and corporeal possession of the Church of . . . with all the rights, profits, and appurtenances thereof.

And after the Incumbent has entered the Church he shall continue:

The Lord preserve your going out and your coming in from this time forth for evermore. Amen.

A Churchwarden shall then present the keys of the Church and Parsonage House, together with the Inventory or Terrier of the Church.

Thereafter the Incumbent shall toll the bell to signify his taking possession; and then with his procession shall go to the Font to join the Bishop there.

If there be no Induction, the Bishop, the Archdeacon, the Incumbent and Churchwardens shall proceed during the singing of the Psalm to the Font.

THE COMMENDATIONS

The Psalm (and the Induction, if there be one) ended, and the Congregation having turned towards the Font, there shall be said:

At the Font

Archdeacon: Our Saviour Christ saith 'Go ye therefore and teach all nations, baptizing them in the Name of the Father, and of the Son, and of the Holy Ghost; teaching them to observe all things whatsoever I have commanded you; and, lo, I am with you alway, even unto the end of the world.'

Bishop (addressing the Incumbent standing before him, and so throughout): Be thou diligent in admonishing parents that they bring their children to Baptism, and in seeking out and leading unbaptized persons into the fellowship of Christ's family: and be thou careful to teach and to prepare for Confirmation by the Bishop those who have been baptized.

Incumbent: I will so do, the Lord being my helper.

The Churchwardens shall conduct the Bishop to the Chancel. They, and the congregation, having turned towards the Sanctuary again, they shall remain standing at the entrance to the Chancel while the Bishop moves to Prayer-Desk, Lectern, and Pulpit.

At the Prayer-Desk

Archdeacon: 'I exhort,' said the Apostle, 'that, first of all, supplications, prayers, intercessions, and giving of thanks, be made for all men; for kings, and for all that are in authority; that we may lead a quiet and peaceable life in all godliness and honesty. For this is good and acceptable in the sight of God our Saviour, who will have all men to be saved, and to come unto the knowledge of the truth.'

Bishop: Be thou faithful in public and private prayer, and zealous and reverent in the ordering of the worship of God's House.

Incumbent: I will, the Lord being my helper.

At the Lectern

Archdeacon: 'All Scripture is given by inspiration of God, and is profitable for doctrine, for reproof, for correction, for instruction in righteousness; that the man of God may be perfect, thoroughly furnished unto all good works.'

Bishop: Wilt thou be ever mindful of the solemn promise made at thy Ordination to study and read God's holy Word and to instruct the people from the same?

Incumbent: I will, the Holy Spirit of God being my guide.

At the Pulpit

Archdeacon: 'We preach not ourselves, but Christ Jesus our Lord; and ourselves your servants for Jesus' sake. For God who commanded light to shine out of darkness, hath shined in our hearts to give the light of the knowledge of the glory of God in the face of Jesus Christ.'

Bishop: Be thou faithful and resolute to declare the Word of God, and ever diligent in teaching and exhorting both them that are within and them that are without, according to the promise made at thy Ordination.

Incumbent: God helping me, I will so endeavour.

At the Sanctuary

Then the Churchwardens shall conduct the Bishop to the Sanctuary, and the Bishop with the Archdeacon and the Incumbent shall proceed to the Holy Table, where the Archdeacon shall say:

'The cup of blessing which we bless, is it not the communion of the Blood of Christ? The bread which we break, is it not the communion of the Body of Christ? For we being many are one bread and one body; for we are all partakers of that one bread. As often as ye eat this bread and drink this cup, ye do show the Lord's death till he come.'

Bishop: Be thou reverent and frequent in the celebration of the Holy Communion of the Body and Blood of Christ; and as thou art partaker of the grace of life through death, so by thy life out-poured for others do thou manifest his glory, who hath redeemed thee by his Cross and will renew thee by his Spirit.

And the Incumbent shall answer:

Amen and Amen. By this Sacrament and Service be known to all men the exceeding love of God.

Then the Archdeacon, turning to the people, shall say:

The Lord Jesus saith, 'He that receiveth whomsoever I send receiveth me; and he that receiveth me receiveth him that sent me.

By this shall all men know that ye are my disciples, if ye have love one toward another.'

Bishop: I charge and exhort you, brethren, to pray continually for this your Minister, who is set over you in the Lord, and to help him forward in all the duties of his holy calling. Bear ye one another's burdens, and so fulfil the law of Christ.

Then shall the Bishop take the Incumbent by his right hand and set him in his stall, saying:

We do set you, brother, in the customary stall of the incumbent of this parish. May God be with you in work and in worship. And may you apprehend that for which you have been apprehended by Christ Jesus. Amen.

[*All kneel*]

Then shall the Incumbent and all the Congregation kneel in silent prayer for a space, after which the new Incumbent alone shall begin the Lord's Prayer, the Congregation joining at the words, For thine is the Kingdom.

Minister: Our Father, which art in heaven,
　　　　　　Hallowed be thy Name;
　　　　　　Thy kingdom come;
　　　　　　Thy will be done;
　　　　　　　In earth as it is in heaven.
　　　　Give us this day our daily bread.
　　　　And forgive us our trespasses,
　　　　As we forgive them that trespass against us.
　　　　And lead us not into temptation;
　　　　　　But deliver us from evil.

Minister and People: For thine is the kingdom,
The power, and the glory,
For ever and ever. Amen.

HYMN

BISHOP'S ADDRESS

HYMN

during which a Collection shall be taken for such object as the Bishop may direct.

Then having presented the offering, the Bishop shall turn to the people and say (the Incumbent kneeling before him):

The Lord be with you;
Answer: And with thy spirit.
Let us pray.

O Almighty God, who makest us to will and to do of thy good pleasure: give thy servant grace truly to perform the solemn vows and promises made by him; and grant that he may be a faithful dispenser of thy holy Word and Sacraments, and a godly example to the people committed to his charge; so that, this life ended, they with him may be partakers of thy heavenly kingdom; through Jesus Christ our Lord. *Amen.*

Then shall the Bishop first bless the Incumbent.

The God of peace, who brought again from the dead our Lord Jesus, that great shepherd of the sheep, through the blood of the everlasting covenant: Make thee perfect in every good work to do his will, working in thee that which is well-pleasing in his sight; through Jesus Christ, to whom be glory for ever and ever. *Amen.*

And thereafter shall he bless the people.

THE COMMISSIONING OF A SUFFRAGAN OR ASSISTANT BISHOP

This Ceremony may take place during a statutory service in the Cathedral, or on a week-day when the full Chapter and the Rural Deans and other clergy can attend. It may appropriately be followed by the Holy Communion.

When all are in their places, the Bishop to be appointed standing before the Bishop of the Diocese on his throne, there shall be said by all together or sung,

Psalm 67

Thereafter the Bishop from his throne shall say:

May God in all things be glorified;

Assistant Bishop: Through Jesus Christ our Lord.

Bishop: He hath remembered his mercy and truth toward the house of Israel;

Assistant Bishop: And all the ends of the world have seen the salvation of our God.

Bishop: Let them give thanks whom the Lord hath redeemed;

Assistant Bishop: And gathered them out of the lands, from the east and from the west.

Bishop: Grace, mercy, peace from God the Father and Christ Jesus our Lord be with thee;

Assistant Bishop: And with thy spirit. Amen.

Then shall all kneel and, after a silence, the Dean shall offer the prayers following:

V. The Lord is nigh unto them that are of a contrite heart;

R. And will save such as be of a humble spirit.

O Lord God, our Creator, Saviour, and Strength, who hast made it thy highest glory to come down to the lowest part of our need; turn our souls, we beseech thee, to that constant beholding and full worship of thee, which shall abase them in their own sight and exalt them in thine, O Father, Son, and Holy Spirit, blessed for evermore. *Amen.*

V. We are the people of his pasture;

R. And the sheep of his hand.

O Lord God, who hast gathered thy children together in the family of thy Holy Catholic Church, grant that the fire of thy love may burn up in us all things that displease thee, and make us fit for the service of thy Kingdom; through Jesus Christ our Lord. *Amen.*

V. Jesus said, Lo I am with you alway;

R. Even unto the end of the world.

Almighty God, who by thy Son Jesus Christ didst give to thy holy Apostles many excellent gifts, and didst charge them to feed thy flock; Give grace, we beseech thee, to all Bishops, the Pastors of thy Church, that they may diligently preach thy Word, and duly administer the godly discipline thereof; and grant to the people that they may obediently follow the same; that all may receive the crown of everlasting glory; through Jesus Christ our Lord. *Amen.*

THE LESSON

St. John 21. 15–19, as appointed in the Order for the Consecration of Bishops.

Thereafter the Bishop shall commend the newly appointed Bishop to the Congregation and welcome him to the Diocese.

This done he shall invite the Chancellor of the Diocese to read the Commission of the appointment of the Bishop and with the Registrar to administer the oaths. (If the suffragan or assistant Bishop is also to be made a member of the Cathedral Chapter then legal formalities for this may be included here.) After these have been duly signed the two Bishops shall proceed to the Sanctuary before the High Altar.

All, kneeling down, shall sing,

Come, Holy Ghost, our souls inspire.

That ended, standing before the Holy Table the Bishop shall say these prayers from the Order for the Consecration of Bishops:

Almighty God, and most merciful Father, who of thine infinite goodness hast given thine only and dearly beloved Son Jesus Christ, to be our Redeemer, and the Author of everlasting life; who, after he had made perfect our Redemption by his death, and was ascended into heaven, poured down his gifts abundantly upon men, making some Apostles, some Prophets, some Evangelists, some Pastors and Doctors, to the edifying and making perfect his Church; Grant, we beseech thee, to this thy servant such grace, that he may evermore be ready to spread abroad thy Gospel, the glad tidings of reconciliation with thee; and use the authority given him, not to destruction, but to salvation; not to hurt, but to help: so that as a wise and faithful servant, giving to thy family their portion in due season, he may at last be received into everlasting joy; through Jesus Christ our Lord, who with thee and the Holy Ghost liveth and reigneth, one God, world without end. *Amen.*

Most merciful Father, we beseech thee to send down upon this thy servant thy heavenly blessing; and so endue him with thy Holy Spirit, that he, preaching thy Word, may not only be earnest to reprove, beseech, and rebuke with all patience and doctrine; but also may be to such as believe a wholesome example, in word, in conversation, in love, in faith, in chastity, and in purity; that, faithfully fulfilling his course, at the latter day he may receive the crown of righteousness laid up by the Lord the righteous Judge, who liveth and reigneth, one God, with the Father and the Holy Ghost, world without end. *Amen.*

And he shall bless his colleague, saying,

The God of peace who brought again from the dead our Lord Jesus, that great shepherd of the sheep, through the blood of the everlasting covenant, make you perfect in every good work to do his will, working in you that which is well-pleasing in his sight, through Jesus Christ; to whom be the glory for ever and ever. *Amen.*

THE KISS OF PEACE

Then the Suffragan or Assistant Bishop having stood up, the Diocesan Bishop shall continue,

O Lord Jesus Christ, who didst say to thine Apostles, Peace I leave with you, my peace I give unto you; regard not our sins, but the faith of thy Church; and vouchsafe to grant unto her peace and unity according to thy will: for thou livest and reignest world without end. *Amen.*

Then turning to the other Bishop he shall give him the Kiss of Peace, with the words,

Pax tibi et ecclesiae Dei

and the other shall respond,

Et cum spiritu tuo.

After a silence the hymn following shall be sung,

Happy are they, they that love God.

The Assistant Bishop, having moved to the Holy Table, shall say this prayer for the diocese:

Holy Father, Almighty and Everlasting God, who hast in the fullness of time through thy Eternal Son reconciled mankind unto thyself, and after his glorious Resurrection and Ascension didst manifest through his holy Church thy love and righteous will towards all men: Let thy Holy Spirit descend with seven-fold power upon the Bishop, clergy, and people of this diocese. Enable us so to worship that men may know and adore the beauty of thy holiness; to live and labour that we may declare the greatness of thy love; to learn and teach that we may be faithful stewards of thy truth. And grant that, encompassed by those who are now in felicity, and strengthened by the fullness of thy power, we may enter into the joy of thy dear Son, to whom with thee and the Holy Spirit we ascribe honour, praise, and dominion now and evermore. *Amen.*

And he shall bless the Bishop of the Diocese, the Chapter, and the Congregation, saying:

The peace of God, which passeth all understanding, keep your hearts and minds in the knowledge and love of Jesus Christ our Lord;

And the blessing of God Almighty be upon you and remain with you always. *Amen.*

THE COLLATION AND INSTALLATION OF A CANON OF A CATHEDRAL

The Form may be used for the Collation of an Archdeacon in its entirety, except that for canon *or* canonry, *the words* archdeacon *or* archdeaconry *will have to be substituted.*

When the appointment belongs to the Bishop by virtue of his bishopric, the act of Institution is called a Collation.

At the time appointed, the members of the Chapter being in their places, there shall be said or sung Deus Misereatur.

God be merciful unto us, and bless us: and shew us the light of his countenance, and be merciful unto us:

That thy way may be known upon earth: thy saving health among all nations.

Let the people praise thee, O God: yea, let all the people praise thee.

O let the nations rejoice and be glad: for thou shalt judge the folk righteously, and govern the nations upon earth.

Let the people praise thee, O God: yea, let all the people praise thee.

Then shall the earth bring forth her increase: and God, even our own God, shall give us his blessing.

God shall bless us: and all the ends of the world shall fear him.

Glory be to the Father, and to the Son: and to the Holy Ghost;

As it was in the beginning, is now, and ever shall be: world without end. Amen.

Then the Canon-elect, accompanied by the Dean or Provost and the Registrar, standing before him, the Bishop shall say:

May God in all things be glorified;

And the Chapter shall answer:

Through Jesus Christ our Lord. *Amen.*

Then shall the Bishop say:

Brethren and people, it is our good purpose to appoint and collate the Reverend *A.B.*, Clerk, who has been properly commended to us, to the Canonry of . . . in this Cathedral Church. But first it is required by the Church's law and the statutes of this Cathedral that he should in our presence and before you make certain declarations and take Oaths of Allegiance to Her Majesty the Queen and of canonical Obedience to the Bishop of the Diocese. Wherefore, let these be taken and made.

The congregation being seated, the Canon-elect shall make the declaration of assent and the declaration against simony (if not previously made) and take the oaths on a copy of the Gospel.

Thereafter, all standing, the Bishop shall move to a chair before the Holy Table and shall bid the people to prayer, saying:

Let us pray for our Cathedral and Diocese, and for this our brother that God in his mercy may give him grace and power to keep the vows that he has now made and to fulfil the duties of the office to which he has been called.

All kneeling, then shall be said:

Lord, have mercy upon us.
Answer: Christ, have mercy upon us.
Lord, have mercy upon us.

Almighty and everlasting God, by whose Spirit the whole body of the Church is governed and sanctified; receive our supplications and prayers, which we offer before thee for all estates of men in thy Holy Church, that every member of the same, in his vocation and ministry, may truly and godly serve thee; through our Lord and Saviour Jesus Christ. *Amen.*

O Almighty God, who hast built thy Church upon the foundation of the Apostles and Prophets, Jesus Christ himself being the head corner-stone; grant us so to be joined together in unity of spirit by their doctrine; that we may be made an holy temple acceptable unto thee; through Jesus Christ our Lord. *Amen.*

Almighty God, giver of all good things, who by thy Holy Spirit hast appointed divers orders of ministers in the Church; mercifully behold thy servant *A.B.* now called to this office and administration in the same; and so replenish him with the truth of thy doctrine, and adorn him with innocency of life, that, both by word and good example, he may faithfully serve thee in this office, to the glory of thy Name, and the edification of thy Church; through the merits of our Saviour Jesus Christ, who liveth and reigneth with thee and the Holy Ghost, world without end. *Amen.*

O Lord, who hast taught us that all our doings without charity are nothing worth: Send thy Holy Ghost, and pour into our hearts that most excellent gift of charity, the very bond of peace and of all virtues, without which whosoever liveth is counted dead before thee: Grant this for thine only Son Jesus Christ's sake. *Amen.*

Then may be sung, kneeling, the hymn:

Come, Holy Ghost, our souls inspire

The Canon-elect kneeling before the Bishop, and the congregation meantime standing, the Bishop shall read the Deed of Collation, and giving it to him he shall add:

Receive your cure my care; In the Name of the Father, the Son, and the Holy Spirit. Amen.

And he shall bless him:

The God of peace, that brought again from the dead our Lord Jesus, that great Shepherd of the sheep, through the blood of the everlasting covenant; make thee perfect in every good work to do His will, working in thee that which is well pleasing in His sight, through Jesus Christ, to whom be glory for ever and ever. Amen.

Thereafter the Bishop shall require the Dean or Provost to install the new Canon, who shall make such declaration as is required by the Constitution of the Cathedral.

In the Name of the Father, and of the Son, and of the Holy Ghost, I, *A.B.*, being now duly appointed to be a Canon of this Cathedral Church of . . ., do solemnly declare that I will faithfully observe and keep the Statutes and By-laws thereof; that I will, to the utmost of my power, defend and maintain the possessions, privileges, and rights of this Church; that I will forward and promote such works as may fitly be done therein for the service of God and for the benefit of his Church in this Diocese, and that, if I shall be called and appointed to any office or administration for such purpose, I will be ready to undertake and fulfil the same to the best of my ability.

The Dean or Provost shall then conduct the Canon to his stall, and, taking his right hand, shall say:

In the Name of God. Amen.

I, *D.C.*, of this Cathedral Church, together with these my brethren, receive thee, *A.B.*, as a brother and Canon, in the Name of the Father, and of the Son, and of the Holy Ghost. Amen.

Then, causing the Canon to be seated in his stall, the Dean or Provost shall say:

We install thee, brother, into the stall assigned to thy Canonry, and do effectually induct thee into the real, actual, and corporal possession of the same, with all and singular its rights, members, and appurtenances.

The Lord preserve thy going out and thy coming in from this time forth for evermore. *Amen.*

Then shall be sung the hymn:

Pray that Jerusalem may have . . .

Thereafter, if there be no address, all shall kneel and the Bishop shall say:

Grant, O Lord, we beseech thee, that the course of this world may be so peacefully ordered by thy governance that thy Church may joyfully serve thee in all godly quietness; through Jesus Christ our Lord. *Amen.*

O Lord God, who hast gathered thy children together in the family of thy Holy Catholic Church, grant that the fire of thy love may burn up in us all things that displease thee, and make us fit for the service of thy Kingdom; through Jesus Christ our Lord. *Amen.*

THE BLESSING

THE ADMISSION OF A CHANCELLOR

It is desirable that members of the Legal Profession in the City and Diocese should be invited to attend as well as the Clergy and Laity of the Diocese. The Form should be preceded by Evensong from the opening Response to the Third Collect.

Proper Psalms: 15 *and* 119.105–12.
First Lesson: Isaiah 9.2–9.
Second Lesson: St. Matthew 7.1–12.

After the Collect for the Day this Prayer shall be said,

O God, by whose spirit men are taught to discern good and evil, and before whose throne at the last each must render his account, guide with thy pure wisdom those who make our laws, and enable, we beseech thee, those who administer the same to lay aside all private interests, prejudices, and partial affections, that justice and equity, mercy and truth may abound among us, and thy people be united in Christian love and charity one towards another; through Jesus Christ our Lord. *Amen.*

HYMN

Judge eternal, throned in splendour,
    Lord of lords and King of kings,
With thy living fire of judgement
    Purge this realm of bitter things:
Solace all its wide dominion
    With the healing of thy wings.

Still the weary folk are pining
    For the hour that brings release:
And the city's crowded clangour
    Cries aloud for sin to cease;
And the homesteads and the woodlands
    Plead in silence for their peace.

Crown, O God, thine own endeavour:
    Cleave our darkness with thy sword:
Feed the faint and hungry heathen
    With the richness of thy Word:
Cleanse the body of this empire
    Through the glory of the Lord.

SERMON

by the Lord Bishop of the Diocese.

[All remain standing]

Thereafter, the Bishop being set in his chair at the entrance to the Sanctuary, the Registrar shall present the Chancellor-designate to the Bishop, saying:

Right Reverend Father in God, I present unto you *A.B.*, to be admitted to the office of Chancellor of this your diocese of . . .

The Bishop, having signified his willingness, shall say:

> The Lord be with you;
> *Answer:* And with thy spirit.
> *Bishop:* Let us pray.

[All kneel]

Eternal God, who art the righteous and merciful Judge of all mankind, enlighten the minds and purify the hearts of those appointed to minister justice between man and man, to clear the innocent and correct the guilty, that by the illumination of thy Holy Spirit they may execute their office for the benefit of this realm and people and to the honour and praise of thy Name; through Jesus Christ our Lord. *Amen.*

Bishop: Blessed is the man whose trust is in thee;

Answer: And in whose heart are thy ways.

Bishop: Almighty and everlasting God, from whom cometh every good and perfect gift, and without whose sufficient grace none can do justly and love mercy: give to thy servant, *A.B.*, now called to exercise judgement and minister justice in this Diocese, the spirit of wisdom and understanding, the spirit of counsel and might, the spirit of knowledge and of the fear of thee: and grant, we beseech thee, that he may alway boldly, discreetly, and in true charity fulfil his sacred duties; through

Jesus Christ our Lord, to whom be praise and glory evermore. *Amen.*

[All sit]

Bishop: Let the Oaths be taken and subscribed.

Then shall the Registrar administer the Oath of Allegiance, the Oath required by the Canon, and the Subscription to the Thirty-Nine Articles:

I, *A.B.*, do sincerely promise and swear that I will be faithful and bear true allegiance to Her Majesty Queen Elizabeth II, her heirs and successors according to law.

So help me God.

I, *A.B.*, do, before I enter into or execute the Office of Principal Official and Judge and Chancellor of the Consistory Court of the Right Reverend Father in God, *N.*, by Divine Permission Lord Bishop of . . ., and of his successors, Bishops of . . ., and of Vicar General in Spirituals of the Bishoprick of . . ., Swear that I will, to the utmost of my understanding, deal uprightly and justly in the execution of the said office, without respect or favour or reward.

So help me God and these Holy Gospels.

I, *A.B.*, in order to my being admitted to exercise and execute the Office of Principal Official and Judge and Chancellor of the Consistory Court of the Right Reverend Father in God, *N.*, by Divine Permission Lord Bishop of . . ., and Vicar General in Spirituals of the Bishoprick of . . ., do assent to the Thirty-Nine Articles of Religion, concluded and agreed upon at the Convocation held in London in the year of our

Lord One Thousand Five hundred and Sixty-two, this
. . . day of . . . in the year of our Lord. . . .

[All stand]

*The Chancellor having signed such Oaths and Subscription,
shall kneel to receive the Patent and Seisin of his Office, and
the Bishop shall say:*

To All Christian People, *N.*, by Divine Permission
Lord Bishop of . . ., Sendeth Greeting in the Lord
Everlasting: Know ye, that we, the said Bishop, for
divers true, good, just and lawful causes and considera-
tions us hereunto specially moving, Do give, commit
and grant unto our well beloved in Christ, *A.B.*,* (in
whose fidelity, learning, uprightness, good morals and
diligence, care and industry in business, We fully con-
fide), the Office of our Chancellor or Vicar General in
Spirituals, and Official Principal in and throughout our
whole Diocese and Jurisdiction of . . ., now void and
devolved into our hands†, the duties, privileges and
appurtenances of which Office are fully set forth and
prescribed in our Letters Patent, which we now present
and deliver unto the said *A.B.*, he having first in our
presence taken such Oaths, and made and Subscribed
such Declarations, as are in such cases required.

*Then shall the Bishop hand the Patent and Seisin of the Office
saying:*

Brother, I deliver to you your Patent as Vicar General
of the Bishop and Official Principal of the Consistory
Court of this Diocese.

* *Here may be added words of description, as* Esquire, Master of Arts.
† *Here may be added such words as* by the death (resignation) of . . .

And laying his hand on the head of the Chancellor, he shall bless him, saying:

[*All stand*]

The Lord bless thee and keep thee: the Lord cause his face to shine upon thee and be gracious unto thee: the Lord lift up the light of his countenance upon thee and give thee peace. And the blessing of God Almighty, Father, Son, and Holy Spirit, be upon thee to give thee wisdom, fidelity, patience, and love all thy days and in all thy works. *Amen.*

HYMN

O God of truth, whose living word
    Upholds whate'er hath breath,
Look down on thy creation, Lord,
    Enslaved by sin and death.

Set up thy standard, Lord, that we
    Who claim a heavenly birth
May march with thee to smite the lies
    That vex thy groaning earth.

Ah! would we join that blest array,
    And follow in the might
Of him, the Faithful and the True,
    In raiment clean and white!

We fight for truth! we fight for God!
    Poor slaves of lies and sin;
He who would fight for thee on earth
    Must first be true within.

Then, God of truth, for whom we long—
    Thou who wilt hear our prayer—
Do thine own battle in our hearts,
    And slay the falsehood there.

> Yea, come! then, tried as in the fire,
>   From every lie set free,
> Thy perfect truth shall dwell in us,
>   And we shall live in thee.

[All kneel]

The Bishop shall bless the people, first saying:

O Lord Jesus Christ, thou merciful judge and loving Saviour, who didst come to reprove with equity for the meek of the earth, look with pity upon thy Church; where it is corrupt cleanse it; where it is amiss correct it; where it is at variance unite it; where it is faithful confirm it, to the glory of thy Name who, with the Father and the Holy Spirit, livest and reignest, one God, world without end. *Amen.*

THE BLESSING

THE COMMISSIONING AND LICENSING OF A DEACONESS OR WOMAN WORKER

NEW CANON APPROVED BY THE CONVOCATIONS
'No woman, being a communicant member of the Church, is qualified to be licensed by a Bishop unless she has received a training approved by the Church and has satisfied duly appointed examiners of her knowledge of the Bible, Doctrine and Pastoralia or has passed some other examination approved by the Bishop as of equivalent standard.'

Before the Service each person to be commissioned or licensed shall, in the presence of the Bishop by whom she is to be so commissioned or licensed or of the Commissary of the such Bishop, make and subscribe the declarations following:

(a) I, *A.B.*, assent to the Book of Common Prayer, and

D.S.B.–E

I believe the doctrine of the Church of England, as therein set forth, to be agreeable to the Word of God.

(b) I, *A.B.*, will give due obedience to the Bishop of ... and his successors in all things lawful and honest.

This form may be used after the third Collect at Matins or Evensong, or as a separate service.

HYMN

Come, Holy Ghost, our souls inspire

SERMON *or* ADDRESS

(This may be given here or before the last hymn)

Thereafter, the Bishop being seated at the entrance to the sanctuary, the person or persons to be commissioned and licensed shall stand out before him and be presented by the Head Deaconess or Secretary of the Board of Women's Work, who shall say:

Reverend Father in God, I present unto you these persons to be commissioned as Women Workers in the Church of England and to be licensed to serve within this Diocese of . . . .

The Bishop: Has full inquiry been made touching their life and conversation and have they been duly instructed in the Church's faith and discipline, and fully trained for the work they will have to do?

Answer: This has been carefully done, and the Board of Women's Work commends them for your Commissioning.

Then, addressing the Congregation assembled, the Bishop shall say:

These are they whom, after due inquiry and examination, we purpose to commission and license, that they may minister in Christ's name and teach in the place (*or* office) where they have been appointed to serve. And that you may know their resolve and that they be made the more mindful of their calling they shall now answer those questions that we now put to them in the name of our Lord Jesus Christ and his Church.

Then he shall examine the candidates, standing before him, after this manner:

Do you trust that you are moved by the Holy Spirit to take upon you the service of our Lord Jesus Christ in his Church?

Answer: I trust so.

The Bishop: Do you believe the Christian faith as it is declared in the Holy Scriptures and in the Book of Common Prayer?

Answer: I do.

The Bishop: Will you endeavour, by the help of God, to fulfil the work committed to you with faithfulness and diligence, ever seeking to love our Lord with your whole heart and to witness to him in word and deed?

Answer: I will so do, by the help of God.

The Bishop: Will you maintain and set forwards quietness and peace and love among all people, and especially in the congregation where you serve?

Answer: I will so do, the Lord being my helper.

The Bishop: Will you reverently obey the Bishop and them to whom the charge and government over you is committed in the Church?

Answer: I will so do, the Lord being my helper.

THE COMMISSIONING

Then shall the Bishop, standing up, say:

May the Holy Spirit, who has given you the will to do these things, grant you strength and power to perform the same: through Jesus Christ our Lord, to whom be the glory evermore. *Amen.*

Then, all kneeling, silence shall be kept for a space, after which he shall say the following prayers:

Look graciously, O Holy Spirit, upon these thy servants and grant them for their hallowing, thoughts that pass into prayer, prayer that passes into love, and love that passes into life with thee for ever. *Amen.*

Almighty and everlasting God, by whose spirit the whole body of the Church is governed and sanctified; receive our supplications and prayers, which we offer before thee for all persons in thy holy Church, that every member of the same, in his vocation and ministry, may truly and godly serve thee; through our Lord and Saviour, Jesus Christ. *Amen.*

Then shall each candidate in turn kneel before the Bishop, who shall deliver unto her the New Testament saying:

N., Receive this Book in token of your Commission to execute the duties and charge of a Woman Worker in the Church of England. The Lord bless you and empower you now and always. *Amen.*

THE LICENSING

Then shall the Bishop proceed to license them to serve in the Diocese, and likewise any others to be licensed who already hold their Commission, first saying this prayer:

O God, the God of all goodness and of all grace, who art

worthy of a greater love than we can either give or understand, fill our hearts with such love towards thee that
nothing may seem too hard for us to do or suffer in
obedience to thy will; and grant that thus loving thee, we
may become daily more like unto thee, and finally enter
the joy of thy eternal life; through Jesus Christ our Lord.
Amen.

Then he shall give to each in turn her Licence saying:

N., Receive your Licence to work in the parish of . . .,
in the name of the Father, and of the Son, and of the Holy
Spirit. *Amen.*

The Bishop: The Lord be with you;

Answer: And with thy spirit.

*Then all shall join in the Lord's Prayer, and thereafter say
together:*

Teach us, good Lord, to serve thee as thou deservest; to
give and not to count the cost; to fight and not to heed the
wounds; to toil and not to seek for rest; to labour and not to
ask for any reward, save that of knowing that we do thy
will, O Lord our God. Amen.

And the Bishop shall bless them in these words:

The God of hope fill you with all joy and peace in
believing, that you may abound in hope through the power
of the Holy Spirit.

And all shall say, Amen.

HYMN

SERMON *or* ADDRESS

(*if not already spoken*)

Before the Blessing the Bishop shall say this prayer for Deaconesses and Women Workers:

O Lord, without whom our labour is but lost and with whom the weak go forth as the mighty: Be present to guide and prosper the work of women in thy Church that they may be enabled to render unto thee their fullest service; and, we beseech thee, give to them a pure intention, patient faith, sufficient success upon earth, and the joy of thy Kingdom in heaven; through Jesus Christ our Lord. *Amen.*

THE BLESSING

THE ADMISSION AND LICENSING OF A READER

HYMN

SERMON

The Sermon ended, these verses from Psalm 119 shall be said antiphonally by all present (vv. 89–96):

O Lord, thy word: endureth for ever in heaven.

Thy truth also remaineth from one generation to another: thou hast laid the foundation of the earth, and it abideth.

They continue this day according to thine ordinance: for all things serve thee.

If my delight had not been in thy law: I should have perished in my trouble.

I will never forget my commandments: for with them thou hast quickened me.

I am thine, O save me: for I have sought thy commandments.

The ungodly laid wait for me to destroy me: but I will consider thy testimonies.

I see that all things come to an end: but thy commandment is exceeding broad.

Glory be to the Father, and to the Son: and to the Holy Ghost;

As it was in the beginning, is now, and ever shall be: world without end. Amen.

ADMISSION OF A READER

The person or persons to be admitted shall then be presented by the Warden or the Honorary Secretary of the Readers' Association to the Bishop, or his deputy, seated before the Sanctuary, saying:

Reverend Father in God, I present unto you these persons to be admitted Readers in the Church of England.

The Bishop: Are the persons you present duly commended as men of good life and honest faith?

Answer: They are so commended by those who know them.

The Bishop: Are you well satisfied that they are able to read the services of the Church plainly, audibly, and reverently?

Answer: We are.

The Bishop: Have they been found on examination by those appointed by us to possess a sufficient knowledge of the Holy Scriptures and of the doctrine and worship of the Church of England as set forth in the Book of Common Prayer, both to teach and to preach if they become so licensed?

Answer: We have examined them and think them so to be.

Then shall the Bishop say to those presented and standing before him:

Will you severally make the Declarations required of those to be admitted Readers.

The candidates shall make the declaration following:

I., *A.B.*, about to be admitted to the Office of a Reader in the Church, do hereby declare as follows: I have been baptized and confirmed, and I am a regular communicant of the Church of England. I assent to the Book of Common Prayer, and I believe the doctrine of the Church of England, as therein set forth, to be agreeable to the Word of God. I will give due obedience to the Bishop of . . . and his successors in all things lawful and honest.

Then the Bishop, standing up, shall say to them:

Almighty God, whom truly to know is everlasting life, grant you perfectly to know Jesus Christ to be the Way, the Truth, and the Life, that you may steadfastly walk in the way that leadeth to eternal life. Amen.

Thereafter all shall kneel and the Bishop shall continue:

O Lord, who hast taught us that all our doings without charity are nothing worth; Send thy Holy Ghost, and pour into our hearts that most excellent gift of charity, the very bond of peace and of all virtues, without which whosoever liveth is counted dead before thee: Grant this for thine only Son Jesus Christ's sake. *Amen.*

Almighty and everlasting God, by whose Spirit the whole body of the Church is governed and sanctified; Receive our supplications and prayers, which we offer before thee for all estates of men in thy holy Church, that every member of the same, in his vocation and ministry, may truly and godly serve thee; through our Lord and Saviour Jesus Christ. *Amen.*

Then to each man kneeling he shall deliver the Certificate of Admission and the New Testament or the Prayer Book, saying:

A.B., I admit you to the Office of a Reader in the Church. May the blessing of God Almighty, Father, Son, and Holy Spirit, rest upon you and upon your work done in his Name. *Amen.*

THE LICENSING OF A READER

(*If there is no Admission preceding, the Licensing shall begin with the two prayers above.*)

The Readers to be licensed shall then join those who have been admitted and together they shall stand before the Bishop or his deputy; and the Bishop shall examine them after this manner:

Will you obey the Bishop of the Diocese and those in authority under him in all things pertaining to your Office?

Answer: I will, the Lord being my helper.

The Bishop: Will you endeavour to order your own lives and the lives of your families to strengthen the fellowship of the Church in its witness to the Kingdom of God and the teaching of Jesus Christ?

Answer: I will so endeavour, the Lord being my helper.

The Bishop: Will you work together gladly and peaceably with the incumbent of the parish to which you are appointed or where you live, helping him forward by your prayers, and ministering with him both to them that are within and to them that are without?

Answer: I will, God being my helper.

The Bishop (or Incumbent) presenting the Certificate of Licensing shall say to each man:

A.B., I hereby license you to serve as Reader in the parish of . . . in the name of God, Father, Son, and Holy Spirit. The Lord be with your going out and your coming in from this time forth. *Amen.*

Then shall all kneel and say with the Bishop as an act of dedication the General Thanksgiving:

Almighty God, Father of all mercies, we thine un-worthy servants do give thee most humble and hearty thanks for all thy goodness and loving-kindness to us, and to all men: We bless thee for our creation, preservation, and all the blessings of this life: but above all, for thine inestimable love in the redemption of the world by our Lord Jesus Christ: for the means of grace, and for the hope of glory. And we beseech thee, give us that due sense of all thy mercies, that our hearts may be unfeignedly thankful, and that we shew forth thy praise, not only with our lips, but in our lives; by giving up ourselves to thy service, and by walking before thee in holiness and righteousness all our days; through Jesus Christ our Lord, to whom with thee and the Holy Ghost be all honour and glory, world without end. *Amen.*

And the Bishop (or Incumbent) shall continue:

O Almighty God, who hast built thy Church upon the foundation of the Apostles and Prophets, Jesus Christ him-self being the head corner-stone; Grant us so to be joined together in unity of spirit by their doctrine, that we may be made an holy temple acceptable unto thee; through Jesus Christ our Lord. *Amen.*

And all shall say together:

Unto him who is able to do exceeding abundantly above all that we ask or think, according to the power that worketh in us; unto him be the glory in the Church by Christ Jesus throughout all ages world without end. Amen.

HYMN

Before the Blessing the Bishop or other minister shall say this prayer:

O Lord God, when thou givest to thy servants to endeavour in any great matter, grant us also to know that it is not the beginning but the continuing unto the end until it be thoroughly finished which yields the true glory: through him who for the finishing of thy work laid down his life, our Redeemer, Jesus Christ. *Amen.*

BLESSING

NOTE
It is desirable that Readers should be admitted at the Annual Service of the Readers in the Diocese and also licensed then. A Reader who has previously been admitted may be licensed in his own parish church on a Sunday at Mattins or Evensong after the Third Collect by the Incumbent as set forth above. When a Diocesan Reader has to be licensed the form of the third demand on page 53 will have to be altered.

II

MEMORIALS AND DEDICATIONS

A MEMORIAL IN A CHURCH OF A CHURCHMAN

[All stand]
The Bishop (or Minister), standing before the Memorial, shall say:

Let us make our dedication, in thankfulness, in prayer, and in love.

O God our Father, who hast called us into the fellowship of thy holy Church through Jesus Christ our Lord, we praise thee for those who have been lights of the world in their generation and in whose lives men have seen the likeness of thy mercy and love: Accept, we beseech thee, this memorial of thy servant, *A.B.*, who by thy grace rendered unto thee in this [city and diocese]* true and laudable service, and grant that it may encourage those who come after to honour thee in like manner to the benefit of thy Church and People; through the same Jesus Christ our Lord. *Amen.*   *(page 129).*

In the faith of Jesus Christ, we dedicate this memorial of *A.B.*: in the name of the Father, and of the Son, and of the Holy Spirit. *Amen.*

Whereupon the Memorial shall be uncovered with the words:

To the glory of God and in memory of *A.B. Amen.*

Then shall all say together the Lord's Prayer.

* Or as appropriate.

THE DEDICATION OF A LADY CHAPEL

With slight changes this form can be adapted for a side chapel with another dedication, or for a refurnished sanctuary.

At the close of the hymn, 'Alleluya, sing to Jesus', *the Bishop or Priest, standing within the Sanctuary, shall say:*

Blessed are the pure in heart: for they shall see God.

People: Blessed are the pure in heart: for they shall see God.

V. And when they saw him: they worshipped him.

R. They shall see God.

V. He shall be great; and shall be called the Son of God.

R. Praise be to thee, O Christ.

Bishop: Let us pray:

Almighty Father, Lord of heaven and earth; be pleased, we humbly beseech thee, to accept these gifts of thy children for the service of thy House of Prayer and for the adornment of thy Sanctuary: for all things come of thee and of thine own do we give thee. Grant that what neither art nor costliness can make worthy for thy service may be hallowed by thy blessing; through Jesus Christ our Lord. *Amen.*

In the faith of Jesus, our Lord, we dedicate this Holy Table and its ornaments for the celebration of the blessed Sacrament of his Body and Blood: together with the gifts which make this Chapel [*or* Sanctuary] meet and comely; in the Name of the Father, Son, and Holy Spirit. *Amen.*

Here may the faithful receive the Bread of Life.

People: Amen.

Here may they be renewed in the vision of God.

People: Amen.

Here may they be strengthened to serve thee with gladness.

People: Amen.

Here remembering the Mother of our dear Lord may they be lifted into the communion and fellowship of the Saints.

People: Amen.

Then while the Holy Table is being vested and the candles lit, the People shall kneel down and sing again this verse:

Alleluya, King eternal,
   Thee the Lord of lords we own;
Alleluya, born of Mary,
   Earth thy footstool, heaven thy throne:
Thou within the veil hast entered;
   Robed in flesh, our great High Priest.
Thou on earth both priest and victim
   In the Eucharistic Feast.

And all shall say together the Collect for the Annunciation:

We beseech thee, O Lord, pour thy grace into our hearts; that as we have known the incarnation of thy Son Jesus Christ by the message of an angel, so by his cross and passion we may be brought unto the glory of his resurrection; through the same Jesus Christ our Lord. Amen.

Thereafter the Bishop or Priest shall, if the gifts are a memorial, say a memorial prayer (cf. pp. 15 and 56) and conclude with the prayers following:

O Holy Spirit, spirit of prayer, spirit of the sons of God, move those who shall worship here and thy whole Church to pray for the cause for which the Christ lived and died and with all his saints lives to plead in heaven. *Amen.*

Grant, O Lord, that the ears which have heard the voice of thy songs may be closed to the voice of clamour and dispute, that the eyes which have seen thy great love may also behold thy blessed hope; that the tongues which have sung thy praise may speak thy truth; that the feet which have walked thy courts may walk in the region of light; that the bodies which partake of thy living Body may be restored in newness of life. And for thine unspeakable Gift, all glory be to thee, O Lord most high. *Amen.*

Let the Peace of God abide here continually,
Peace from God our heavenly Father;
Peace from his Son who is our Peace;
Peace from the Holy Spirit, the Comforter. *Amen.*

THE HALLOWING OR CONSECRATION OF A HOLY TABLE

The Bishop, standing before the Holy Table, shall consecrate it, signing the five Crosses upon it, saying:

Almighty God, in whose honour we, thy unworthy servants, do consecrate this Holy Table by the invocation of thy most Holy Name, mercifully and graciously give ear unto the prayer of our lowliness, and grant that the offerings which we make at this Table be unto thee

accept✠able,
well-plea✠sing,
ri✠ch
and hal✠lowed
with the dew of thy Holy Spi✠rit;

that whensoever thy children make their prayer unto thee in this place, thou mayest relieve their distress, heal their sickness, hearken unto their requests, receive their vows, confirm their longing, and grant their petitions; through

our Lord Jesus Christ, who liveth and reigneth with thee
and the Holy Ghost, world without end. *Amen.*

For the celebration of the Holy Sacrament of the Body
and Blood of Christ we consecrate this Table; in the name
of the Father, and of the Son, and of the Holy Ghost.
Amen.

Our Father . . .

(*This act may appropriately be set within the singing of the
hymn,* 'The Church of God a kingdom is', *the last three
verses being sung after the consecration, while the Holy Table
is being vested.*)

THE GIFT OF A CROSS AND CANDLESTICKS

*The first prayers for the blessing of a Rood (see below) are
suitable, also the Collect for Easter Eve. After the dedication
in the faith of Jesus and in the Name of the Trinity, this
prayer may be added:*

Collect before Blessing.

Almighty God, whose most dear Son went not up to joy
but first he suffered pain, and entered not into glory before
he was crucified: Mercifully grant that we walking the way
of the Cross may find it none other than the way of life
and peace: through the same thy Son, Jesus Christ, our
Lord. *Amen.*

A ROOD

Lection: St. John 19. 17–20, 25b–30.
Prayer: Our help is in the Name of the Lord;
Answer: Who has made heaven and earth.

O God, who by the passion of thy well-beloved Son,
Jesus Christ, hast made the instrument of shameful death

to be glorious in all the world: grant us so to glory in the Cross that we may be freed from the bonds of the sins which were the cause of his passion, and may enter into the Life eternal: through the same Jesus Christ, who with thee and the Holy Spirit lives and reigns, one God, blessed for evermore. *Amen.*

Lift up your hearts.

Answer: We lift them up unto the Lord.

We beseech thee, O Lord, Holy Father, Almighty God, that thou wouldest be pleased to be present among us to *bless* this sign of thy redeeming love: that as by the precious death and resurrection of thy Son, Jesus Christ, thy saving health is known to all men, so his Cross and Passion may be for the solace and protection of thy faithful people: through the same Jesus Christ, who lives and reigns with thee and the Holy Spirit, one God, world without end.

Sanctify, O Lord Jesus, this symbol of thy sacred passion and obedience unto death, may it be blessed in the Name of the Father and the Son and the Holy Spirit, to whom be worship and praise. Alleluia. *Amen.*

Concluding Prayer:

O God, who hast exalted the Crucified, thy Son, by a triumphant resurrection: may his triumphs and glories so shine in the eyes of our hearts and minds, that we may more clearly comprehend his sufferings, and more courageously pass through our own: for his sake who with thee and the Holy Spirit liveth and reigneth one God, for ever and ever.

To God the Father who loves us and makes us acceptable in the Beloved: to God the Son who loves us, and looses us from our sins by his Cross: to God the Holy Spirit who sheds the love of God abroad in the hearts of men: to the one true God be praise and glory, world without end. *Amen.*

A BIBLE OR LECTERN

[*All stand*]

V. O Lord, open thou our lips;

R. And our mouths shall shew forth thy praise.

V. Blessed are they that hear the Word of God, and keep it:

R. All the words which the Lord hath said will we do.

V. The Word was made flesh and dwelt among us:

R. Full of grace and truth:

All. Thanks be to God.

[*All sit*]

Hear the testimony of a good disciple written in the Pilgrim's Progress:

'What do you think of the Bible?'
'It is the holy word of God.'
'Is there nothing written therein but what you understand?'
'Yes, a great deal.'
'What do you do when you meet with such places therein that you do not understand?'
'I think God is wiser than I. I pray also that he will please to let me know all therein he knows will be for my good.'

Let us also pray that we may read the Bible wisely and well.

[*All kneel*]

Blessed Lord, who hast caused all Holy Scriptures to be written for our learning; Grant that we may in such wise hear them, read, mark, learn, and inwardly digest them, that by patience and comfort of thy holy Word, we may embrace, and ever hold fast the blessed hope of everlasting life, which thou hast given us in our Saviour Jesus Christ. *Amen.*

And the Priest, putting his hand on the Bible (Lectern), shall continue:

In the faith of our Saviour Jesus Christ, who is the very Word of God, we dedicate this . . . (and in memory of . . .). In the Name of God, Father, Son, and Holy Spirit. *Amen.*

Here by the careful and diligent reading of this holy Book may those who listen and he who reads know thee more truly and love thee more dearly. *Amen.*

May the Spirit, O Lord, who proceedeth from thee illuminate our minds, and, as thy Son hath promised, guide us into all truth. *Amen.*

Unto the only wise God, our Saviour, be glory and majesty, dominion and power, both now and ever. *Amen.*

AN ORGAN

In the Name of God, Father, Son, and Holy Spirit. Amen.

V. O God my heart is ready, my heart is ready: I will sing and give praise with the best member that I have.

R. O God my heart is ready, my heart is ready: I will sing and give praise with the best member that I have.

V. Awaken thou lute and harp: I myself will awake right early.

R. I will sing and give praise with the best member that I have.

V. Let everything that hath breath: praise the Lord.

R. I will sing and give praise with the best member that I have.

V. Glory be to God on high, and on earth peace and good will among men.

R. O God my heart is ready, my heart is ready: I will sing and give praise with the best member that I have.

All. Glory be to the Father, and to the Son, and to the Holy Ghost; As it was in the beginning, is now, and ever shall be, world without end. Amen.

Let us pray.

O God, Source of all beauty, who hast so created man that in music he can voice that which is beyond speech; we praise and thank thee for the commonalty of music in the world, for the music-makers of every race and nation, and for the instruments of music which men have been guided by thy Spirit to fashion: and now mindful how music has enriched the worship of thy Church, we humbly ask thee to accept this Organ and to hallow and bless its use in our worship: through Jesus Christ our Lord, to whom with thee and the Holy Spirit be praise and adoration evermore. *Amen.*

In the faith of Jesus Christ, we dedicate this Organ to the glory of God Almighty. In the Name of the Father, the Son, and the Holy Spirit. *Amen.*

Holy and Eternal God, whose glory Cherubim and Seraphim and all the hosts of heaven proclaim: sanctify and bless, we beseech thee, the music of our worship and all who make it, and grant that the service that we can only offer unworthily here we may enjoy perfectly in thy heavenly Kingdom: through Jesus Christ our Lord. *Amen.*

V. Let the people praise thee, O God;

R. Yea, let all the people praise thee.

Then shall the Organ sound.

Before the Blessing, there shall be sung:

Gloria in excelsis *or* Psalm 150.

and this prayer shall be said:

Grant, O Lord, that the ears which have heard the voice of thy songs may be closed to the sound of clamour and dispute; that the eyes which have seen thy great love may also behold thy blessed hope: that the tongues which have sung thy praise may speak thy truth: that the feet which have walked thy courts may walk in the region of light. And for thine unspeakable gift, even Jesus Christ, all glory be to thee, O Lord most high. *Amen.*

A PEAL OF BELLS

Grace, Mercy, Peace from God the Father and Christ Jesus our Lord be with us all. *Amen.*

Be pleased, O heavenly Father, to accept this gift, for it is of thine own that we give unto thee; bless and hallow these bells that they may continually draw together thy people to the true worshipping of thee; through Jesus Christ our Lord. *Amen.*

In the faith of Jesus Christ we dedicate the bells now

set in the tower of this Church in memory of . . ., in the name of God the Father, Son, and Holy Spirit. *Amen.*

Let us pray.

We praise thee, O God:

Answer: We acknowledge thee to be the Lord.

Grant, O Lord God our Father, that whosoever shall be called by the ringing of these bells to this House of Prayer may enter into thy gates with thanksgiving and into thy courts with praise;

Grant, O Lord, that whosoever by reason of sickness and infirmity is hindered from coming may by their sound be reminded of the prayers of the Church and draw nearer in spirit to Thee;

Grant, O Lord, that all those for whose passing they shall sound may be cleansed from their sins and find the rest and joy of thy Kingdom;

Grant, O Lord, that all those who ring these bells may do it worthily and to thy glory: through Jesus Christ our Lord, to whom with thee and the Holy Spirit be praise, worship, and dominion for evermore. *Amen.*

O God who art the beginning and the end, the source and fulfilment of all that is good and lovely, establish in the hearts of men and in the places where they live beauty for ugliness, love for hatred, truth for the lie. And, we beseech thee, so sustain us in this endeavour, that looking to the City whose builder and maker is God and persevering unto the end, we may be received into thy eternal habitations: through Jesus Christ our Lord. *Amen.*

Unto the King eternal, immortal, invisible, the only wise God, be honour and glory for evermore. *Amen.*

AN INSTALLATION OF LIGHTING

(*This dedication might well be woven into an Evensong*.)

Opening Sentences

God is light: and in him is no darkness at all.

When thy word goes forth: it gives light and understanding to the simple.

Thy word is a lantern to my feet;

R. And a light unto my path.

Proper Psalm:
Psalm 27.

First Lesson:
Isaiah 60.1–5, 11–13, 18–20.

Second Lesson:
St. Matthew 5.13–16 and 6.19–23.

Special Collect:

O God, the Source of life and light, who dost nourish and gladden all things in heaven and earth: shine in our hearts that the darkness of sin and the mists of error being driven away we may walk without stumbling in the way which thou hast prepared for us to walk in: through Jesus Christ our Lord. *Amen.*

The Dedication and the Intercession following take the place of the second group of prayers.

Let us pray.

O Lord Jesus Christ, Son of the living God, the brightness of his Glory and the express image of his person, accept and bless what has been done for the service of this House of Prayer; and be thou the beginning, the increase, and the end of all our work, to the hallowing of thy Name: who with the Father and the Holy Spirit livest and reignest, one God, world without end. *Amen.*

In the faith of Jesus Christ (and in loving memory of . . .) we dedicate this installation of lighting. In the name of the Father, and of the Son, and of the Holy Spirit. *Amen.*

Jesus said: 'Walk while ye have the light lest darkness come upon you: for he that walketh in darkness knoweth not whither he goeth. While ye have light, believe in the light that ye may be the children of light.'

Appropriate subjects of intercession might be:

The blind, and those who work and watch by night;

Those in doubt and trouble (cf. pp. 109, 110);

The spread of the Gospel and the mission of the Church (cf. p. 175).

HYMN

Thou whose almighty Word.

Collect before the Blessing:

Illuminate, O Lord, the darkness of our night with thy celestial brightness, and from the sons of light banish the deeds of darkness: through Jesus Christ, our Lord. *Amen.*

A CHAPEL SET APART FOR YOUNG PEOPLE AND DEDICATED TO YOUTHFUL SAINTS AND MARTYRS

As the procession moves to the Chapel all shall sing from St. Patrick's Breastplate:

I bind unto myself today
   The strong name of the Trinity,
By invocation of the same,
   The Three in One, and One in Three.

I bind unto myself today
  The power of God to hold and lead,
His eye to watch, his might to stay,
  His ear to hearken to my need.
The wisdom of my God to teach,
  His hand to guide, his shield to ward;
The word of God to give me speech,
  His heavenly host to be my guard.

[All sit]
A young person shall read from the Word of God:

Isaiah 40.25–31.

[All then stand]
The Bishop or Minister shall say these prayers and then dedicate the Chapel:

O God who art the light of the minds that know thee and the joy of loving hearts; Grant that the life of thy Church on earth may be so quickened, the wisdom of its leaders so pure, the lives of its members so winning; that the power of the Gospel may be known in all the world and thy love for ever adored; through Jesus Christ, who with thee, O Father, and the Holy Spirit lives and reigns, one God, world without end.

People: Alleluia. Amen.

Grant, O heavenly Father, that the homes of thy children may be an image of thy Kingdom and the care of parents for children and children for parents a likeness of thy wisdom and love: to the praise of Jesus Christ, our Lord.

People: Amen.

In the faith of Jesus Christ we dedicate this Chapel [and the furnishings and ornaments thereof] in honour of his youthful saints and martyrs of every nation and age, who being made strong in the worshipping of God and by the power of the Holy Spirit have faced life and death humbly and unafraid, and now rejoice in his eternal Kingdom. In the Name of the Father, the Son, and the Holy Spirit.

People: Amen.

Here may the young be strengthened in resolve and hope; Here may they be uplifted to walk the way of Jesus with gladness, courage, and tranquillity; to whom be the praise and the glory evermore. *Amen.*

Then shall all kneel and sing or say:

> Christ be with me, Christ within me,
> Christ behind me, Christ before me,
> Christ beside me, Christ to win me,
> Christ to comfort and restore me,
> Christ beneath me, Christ above me,
> Christ in quiet, Christ in danger,
> Christ in hearts of all that love me,
> Christ in mouth of friend and stranger.

Thereafter silence shall be kept during which prayer shall be made that the Church here and everywhere may be made strong in joy, love, sincerity, and in the fellowship of the Holy Spirit.

And the Bishop or Minister shall conclude, saying,

May the benediction of thy Presence, O Lord, rest upon this place and dwell in the hearts of all who shall serve and worship here. Alleluia. Amen.

Then shall all stand and sing again:

> I bind unto myself today
> The strong name of the Trinity
> By invocation of the same,
> The Three in One, and One in Three.

and thereafter go in procession out of the building singing:

either, Ye servants of God, your Master proclaim,

or, He would who valiant be.

THE HALLOWING OF A DWELLING OR CONFERENCE HOUSE OR A COLLEGE HOSTEL OR A PARSONAGE HOUSE

At the Door:

Heavenly Father, who hast given us thy dear Son for our light and salvation; grant us grace to reveal his brightness to the lives of others and to render it back to thee in our own: prosper and protect this undertaking with thy continual blessing and let thy peace and joy be with all who enter by this door; for the sake of Jesus Christ our Lord, who with thee and the Holy Spirit liveth and reigneth, one God, world without end. *Amen.*

On Entering:

Peace be to this house and to all who live and work in it;
Peace to all who enter or go from it;
Peace from God our Father and the Lord Jesus abide here continually.

When the building is for educational and religious purposes these prayers may be used:

Almighty Father, Lord of heaven and earth, from whom cometh every good and perfect gift, be pleased to accept the gifts and labours of many people which have made possible the building, furnishing, and opening of this place: Use it, we beseech thee, for thy purposes, hallow it with thy blessing, and grant that the power of thy love may radiate from it into the lives of many people: through Jesus Christ our Lord. *Amen.*

May the Holy Spirit of God refresh and illuminate the minds of all who shall come here, and as our Lord hath promised lead them into all truth with all charity. *Amen.*

For the Life and Work of the House:

V. Our help is in the Name of the Lord;

R. Who hath made heaven and earth.

O Lord God, who hast commanded that whatsoever we do should be done in thy Name, grant thy spirit of wisdom and love to those on whom rest the ordering and service of this house; give refreshment and good health to those who sojourn here; so that in all things thy Kingdom may be advanced; through Jesus Christ our Lord. *Amen.*

V. Now abideth faith, hope, and charity;

R. And the greatest of these is charity.

O Lord who hast taught us that all our doings without charity are nothing worth; Send thy Holy Spirit and pour into the hearts of those who will meet, speak, and discuss here that most excellent gift of charity, the very bond of peace and of all virtues, without which whosoever liveth is counted dead before thee. Grant this for thine only Son Jesus Christ's sake. *Amen.*

A Dining Room:

V. Whether ye eat or drink or whatsoever ye do;

R. Do all to the glory of God.

O Lord Christ, who in thy earthly life sat at meat with men and women and shared their feasts, and who hast bidden us to pray faithfully for our daily bread; grant that those who partake of meat and drink here may have good fellowship in the enjoyment of these thy gifts; to the praise of thy Name. *Amen.*

A Kitchen:

V. As the body apart from the spirit is dead;

R. Even so faith apart from works.

Almighty God, who hast ordered that our bodies should have to be refreshed with daily food; bless those who shall have the preparing of it in this kitchen; grant them skill and patience to do it well as unto thee, and contentment in the doing of it; that by their service this house may be a happy and a homely place; through thy Son who dwelt in an earthly home. *Amen.*

A Bedroom or Dormitory:

V. I will lay me down in peace;

R. And take my rest.

O Lord God, who neither slumberest nor sleepest but art ever watchful of the creaturely needs of thy children; enfold in thy protecting mercy all who shall sleep here, that they may awake to the new day refreshed in body and spirit to praise thee more gladly who givest all: through Jesus Christ who died and rose again for our salvation. *Amen.*

A Garden:

V. They heard the voice of the Lord God;

R. Walking in the garden in the cool of the day.

Eternal God, who hast made heaven and earth and all that is good and lovely therein, and whose beloved Son in the days of his earthly life found in nature both solace of mind and parables of thy providence; help us to enjoy in like manner our earthly heritage and to reverence all thy works and creatures; and grant, we beseech thee, that men and women tired with their work may here find release from anxiety and the rest of God: through Jesus Christ our Lord. *Amen.*

DEDICATION OF A HOSPITAL UNIT

The Bishop or the Minister who is asked to dedicate and bless shall say:

Let us pray.

Almighty and Everliving God from whom cometh every good and perfect gift, be pleased to accept the thought, the gifts, the skills and labours which have made possible the building and equipping of this hospital unit. According to thy merciful purpose use, we beseech thee, the service of its doctors, surgeons, and nurses [and the work of research that will go forward here]* for the health and wholeness of many people: through Jesus Christ our Lord. *Amen.*

Almighty God, we commend all sufferers to thy loving care, especially those who will come for treatment here. Grant them patience in their distress, cheer and uphold them in mind and body, and grant that by their treatment and care here they may be restored to health and strength: through Jesus Christ our Lord. *Amen.*

Then the Bishop shall dedicate the Unit with these words:

In the faith of Jesus Christ [and in memory of . . .]* we dedicate this . . ., in the name of God, Father, Son, and Holy Spirit. *Amen.*

* To be included if appropriate.

Then shall all say together:

Our Father . . . for ever and ever. *Amen.*

THE BLESSING

AT THE OPENING OF A NEW SCHOOL

The Lord is my light and my salvation: whom then shall I fear?

The earth, O Lord, is full of thy mercy: O teach me thy statutes.

Thy word is a lantern to my feet: and a light unto my paths.

The Lessons:

Jeremiah 9.23–24, *or* Philippians 4.8–9 ('Brethren . . .')

and

St. Matthew 7.24–29 ('Jesus said, . . .')

Let us say together:

Our Father . . .

In the faith of Jesus Christ [and in memory of . . .] we dedicate this School. May it always stand for that which is true, noble, just, and lovely. May the Spirit of the living God illuminate the minds of those who direct its use: and guide into all truth with all charity the teachers and learners who will come to it and go from it so that many hereafter will bless the day when it was opened. The peace of God make it a happy place. *Amen.*

A Prayer for the Builders.

O God who art the beginning and the end of all that is good and lovely, continue thy blessing upon the work of education and upon those who design and build. Establish in the hearts of all people and in the places where they live, beauty for ugliness, love for hatred, truth for the lie; that so thy will may be done on earth. And, we beseech thee, sustain us in this endeavour that looking to that City whose builder and maker is thou, O God, and persevering unto the end, we may be received into thy eternal habitations; through Jesus Christ our Lord. *Amen.*

(The Prayer of St. Chrysostom may be added)

A Blessing or Ascription

A GENERAL PRAYER OF DEDICATION

O Holy Spirit of the living God, proceeding from the Father and the Son, Spirit of truth and love, the Lord and Giver of life, sanctify with thy presence this place of prayer.

Here may the people be drawn into thy fellowship and conquered by thy love; here may the ignorant learn the way of truth, the sinful find pardon, and the weary rest; here may the members of thy Holy Church be strengthened in the bond of peace and righteousness of life, manfully to confess the faith of Christ crucified.

Fulfil the prayers of those who worship here, hallow their praises and enrich their lives; unite them in the service of the Kingdom which hath no end, that in all things and by all men thy name may be adored, Who with the Father and the Son livest and reignest, one God, world without end. *Amen.*

III

OCCASIONAL OFFICES

A THANKSGIVING OF PARENTS AFTER THE BIRTH OF A CHILD*

When the parents have knelt down at the Communion rails, the Minister standing within the Sanctuary, they shall say, with him:

Unto the God and Father of our Lord Jesus Christ from whom cometh every good and perfect gift, be praise, thanksgiving and blessing. *Amen.*

Our Father . . . for ever and ever. Amen.

Then shall they stand and say all together Psalm 121, or part of Psalm 117, as follows:

(The verses are said by Minister and parents alternately, and the refrain and Gloria together)

Together: We will walk before God; in the land of the living.

Minister: I am well pleased: that the Lord hath heard the voice of my prayer;

Answer: That he hath inclined his ear unto me; therefore will I call upon him as long as I live.

---

* A Service on these lines was discussed in the Convocation of York at one time, and amended, but it was not finally revised in committee or presented for approval.

D.S.B.—G

Minister: Gracious is the Lord, and righteous: yea, our God is merciful.

Answer: The Lord preserveth the simple: I was in misery, and he helped me.

Minister: Turn again then unto thy rest, O my soul: for the Lord hath rewarded thee.

Answer: And why? thou hast delivered my soul from death: mine eyes from tears, and my feet from falling.

    Together: I will walk before the Lord: in the land of the living.

Minister: What reward shall I give unto the Lord: for all the benefits that he hath done unto me?

Answer: I will receive the cup of salvation: and call upon the Name of the Lord.

Minister: I will pay my vows now in the presence of all his people: in the courts of the Lord's house;

Answer: Praise the Lord.

    Together: Glory be to the Father and to the Son and to the Holy Ghost: as it was in the beginning, is now, and ever shall be, world without end. We will walk before the Lord; in the land of the living.

Minister: Let us pray.

[*The parents kneel*]

O Almighty Lord and everlasting God, vouchsafe, we beseech thee, to direct, sanctify, and govern both our hearts and bodies in the ways of thy laws and in the works of thy commandments; that through thy most mighty protection both here and ever we may be preserved in body and soul; through our Lord and Saviour Jesus Christ. *Amen.*

Then shall they say this thanksgiving with the Minister, and the Grace following:

Glory be to thee, O God, for thy goodness and mercy, for the skill and care that have brought thy servant through child-birth; for the child that has been born. Grant us so to live that he may have a happy home and grow up to praise thee in thy Church; through Jesus Christ our Saviour and Lord. Amen.

The grace of our Lord Jesus Christ and the love of God and the fellowship of the Holy Spirit be with us and our children now and always. Amen.

The Minister shall give them a Blessing.

This thanksgiving may be said as an alternative to the office of Churching, either before Holy Communion, if the parents are communicants, or before the christening of the baby.

It could also be said by parents in the home beside the new-born babe and would then be a remembrance of the Holy Family at Bethlehem.

THE PUBLIC BAPTISM OF INFANTS

THE REVISED ORDER AND DIRECTIONS APPROVED BY THE CONVOCATION OF YORK IN 1951, WITH SOME AMENDMENTS AFTER EXPERIMENTAL USE

AN HISTORICAL NOTE

In October 1943, the Convocations of Canterbury and York asked their Presidents 'to take the necessary steps to appoint a joint committee to draft *a simpler, more intelligible* Order of Holy Baptism for submission to the Convocations'.

The Committee was duly appointed and after the members in each Convocation had met separately and had joint meetings, the Canterbury members, and especially their chairman, the former Bishop of Exeter, wanted a form much more drastically simplified than the York members envisaged. This difference, combining with the difficulty of meeting owing to flying bombs, resulted by the end of the War in the York members being left to go it alone. We presented our first draft to Convocation in October 1945. The revision of this was considered by the Upper House at three sessions in 1947–8, sent back to the Lower House in 1949, and finally approved by the Full Synod in September 1951, when the President was 'respectfully asked to take what steps he thinks most suitable to enable the revised service of Holy Baptism to be used experimentally in the Church'. In the Upper House in October 1952, the Archbishop stated that in his opinion 'bishops of the province should feel themselves free to allow some of their clergy who wish to do so to use the revised service of Baptism but any such permission given should be only for a given period, and at the end of the time the clergy using the service should report to the bishop as to the suitability of the service as shown by experience. And the use of this service should be reconsidered when the Canon on Lawful Authority is carried through . . .'.

As convener of the drafting committee I made the necessary arrangements for this experiment to be carried out. Several thousand copies of the Service were printed on stiff cards and distributed by eight diocesan bishops to a limited number of incumbents in 1952–3. Reports from these were collected and collated in 1955–6. The Upper House in May 1956 decided that the experiment should cease and the Bishop of Sheffield was asked to report the findings to the Liturgical Commission. This I did through the Dean of York on 20 November 1956. The Dean, speaking in York Convocation on 19 January 1960, said that the reports from the incumbents were 90 per cent. in favour of its adoption—some making useful minor amendments.

After a discussion prolonged over two Sessions in Full Synod on the Report of the Liturgical Commission, the following resolution was agreed: 'That this Convocation having carefully considered and finally approved a revised service for the Baptism of Infants in September 1951 wishes to affirm its preference for this service, subject to minor alterations suggested by its experimental use and by further consideration.' In January 1961, the Convocation, after a long discussion in Full Synod on the Report of the Joint Committee on Baptism and Confirmation, re-affirmed this preference by a vote of seven to nil in the Upper House and by an overwhelming majority in the Lower House.

In the meantime, the late Dean of York, as a member of the Liturgical Commission, had submitted an altered version of the York Service to the Liturgical Commission. He drew attention to these proposed alterations in a memorandum he circulated to Convocation in which he argued in favour of the York Service. He later had the service with his alterations published, but they have not been discussed by Convocation either in Synod or in committee.

———————

The Service printed hereafter and its rubrics are as approved by the York Convocation in 1951, with the change from 'minister' to 'priest' throughout and three emendations in the prayers that were approved after the period of experiment.

THE PUBLIC BAPTISM OF INFANTS

The font shall be set in as spacious and well-ordered sur-roundings as can be compassed. When not in use it must be decently covered; and a reverent care at all times should be given to the seemliness and dignity of its appointments.

It is desirable that Baptism should on due occasion be administered at Morning or Evening Prayer upon Sundays and other Holy Days when the most number of people come together; both that the congregation may testify the receiving of them that be newly baptized into the number of Christ's Church, and also that everyone present may be put in remembrance of his own profession made to God in his baptism.

If the Baptism be held at Morning or Evening Prayer, it shall follow the Second Lesson, and be followed by the second Canticle, Versicles, and the Collects: the Creed, Lesser Litany, and Lord's Prayer being omitted.

Should the disposition of the church and the seating render it appropriate, any part of the service, other than the Blessing of the Water, the naming and the Baptizing of the child, may take place, in the discretion of the minister, at the entrance of the Chancel facing the people.

In case of dangerous illness of the child, no minister being available, a lay person may name the child and pour water upon it, saying:

N. I baptize thee in the Name of the Father, and of the Son, and of the Holy Ghost. Amen.

And then those that are present shall say the Lord's Prayer. And afterwards notice of the Baptism shall be given to the minister of the parish, and the child's name duly entered in the parish register. Further, if the child do live, it shall be brought to the church that it may be received publicly into the congregation.

―――――――

[*Note: To prevent too long standing, especially by those holding the baby, thought should be given and seating arranged so as to allow the congregation, or those who so wish, to sit during a longer part of the service.*]

THE ORDER OF SERVICE
THE PREPARATION

When the people are gathered round the font (which is to be filled with pure water) and the Priest has been assured that the child has not been already baptized, he shall proceed after this manner:

[*All stand*]

Priest: Beloved, you have brought *this child* to be baptized. You are asking for *him* a gift which God alone can give. Our Saviour Christ himself said, None can enter into the kingdom of God, except he be born again of water and of the Holy Ghost. In the sacrament of Holy Baptism, the outward sign of which is washing by water, our heavenly Father promises to give *this child* that which by *his* own nature *he* cannot have, that is to say, new birth as the child of God, the forgiveness of sin, and an inheritance in his eternal kingdom.

That you may be sure of the goodwill of God towards *this child*, hear in the Gospel how the Lord Jesus received the children brought to him.

THE GOSPEL (*St. Mark* 10.13)

They brought young children to Christ that he should touch them; and his disciples rebuked those that brought them. But when Jesus saw it, he was much displeased, and said unto them, Suffer the little children to come unto me, and forbid them not; for of such is the kingdom of God. Verily, I say unto you, whosoever shall not receive the kingdom of God as a little child, he shall not enter therein. And he took them up in his arms, put his hands upon them, and blessed them.

Answer: Praise be to thee, O Christ.

Priest: Let us say together,

Priest and People: Almighty God, our heavenly Father, who by the Baptism of thy well-beloved Son Jesus Christ in the river Jordan didst sanctify water to the mystical washing away of sin; graciously look upon *this child;* embrace *him* with the arms of thy mercy; cleanse and sanctify *him* by thy Holy Spirit; and take *him* into the family of thy Church; that *he* may live in thy love and favour for ever; through Jesus Christ our Lord. Amen.

THE DUTIES OF PARENTS AND GODPARENTS

[*Congregation sits.*
Parents and godparents stand by the font.]

Priest: You are accepting the responsibility of *this child*'s upbringing within the family of Christ's Church. To this end it will be your duty as parents and godparents:

First, to see that *he* is taught the Creed, the Lord's Prayer, the Ten Commandments, as set forth in the Church Catechism, and all other things which a Christian ought to know and believe to his soul's health.

Secondly, to help *him* by your example and your prayers, as well as by your teaching, to be diligent in public worship and in private prayer, to be true and just in all *his* dealings, and to lead a godly and Christian life.

Thirdly, to bring *him* in due time to the bishop to be confirmed; so that *he*, being strengthened with the Holy Spirit, and regularly receiving the Holy Communion of the Body and Blood of Christ, may go forth into the world to serve God faithfully in the fellowship of his Church.

Do you promise, in the presence of God and of this congregation, that you will perform these duties faithfully?

Parents and Godparents: I do.

Priest: God grant you strength and power to do all these things that you have promised.

Answer: Amen.

THE THREE-FOLD PROMISE,
MADE BY THE GODPARENTS

Priest: You who have brought *this child* to be baptized and stand in the presence of God, must now make on *his* behalf the Promises which *he* will renew in *his* own *person* when *he* comes to be confirmed.

Do you, in the name of *this child*, renounce all that is evil, and promise to resist the temptations of the devil, the world, and the flesh, so that you will not follow nor be led by them?

Answer: I do.

Priest: Do you, in the name of *this child*, promise to hold fast the Christian Faith?

Answer: I do.

Then shall all stand and say with the godparents and the Priest the Apostles' Creed:

I believe in God the Father Almighty, Maker of heaven and earth:

And in Jesus Christ his only Son our Lord, Who was

conceived by the Holy Ghost, Born of the Virgin Mary, Suffered under Pontius Pilate, Was crucified, dead and buried, He descended into hell; The third day he rose again from the dead, He ascended into heaven, And sitteth on the right hand of God the Father Almighty; From thence he shall come to judge the quick and the dead.

I believe in the Holy Ghost; The holy Catholick Church; The Communion of Saints; The Forgiveness of sins; The Resurrection of the body; And the Life everlasting. Amen.

Minister: Do you, in the name of *this child*, promise obedience to God's will and commandments?

Answer: I do.

[*All remain standing*]

Priest: O merciful God, grant that *this child* may have power and strength to have victory and to triumph against the devil, the world, and the flesh.

Answer: Amen.

Priest: Grant that, being steadfast in faith, joyful through hope, and rooted in charity, *he* may at the last come to thy heavenly kingdom through thy mercy, O blessed Lord God, who dost live and govern all things, world without end.

Answer: Amen.

THE BLESSING OF THE WATER

Priest: The Lord be with you;
Answer: And with thy spirit.

Priest: Lift up your hearts;
Answer: We lift them up unto the Lord.

Priest: Let us give thanks unto our Lord God;
Answer: It is meet and right so to do.

Priest: It is very meet, right, and our bounden duty that we should give thanks unto thee, O Lord, Holy Father, Almighty, Everlasting God, because thou didst give thy most dearly beloved Son, Jesus Christ, to be made man and to suffer death for the forgiveness of our sins, to bring us out of darkness into his glorious light: who after his mighty resurrection did send his Holy Spirit upon the disciples, giving them commandment to go teach all nations and baptize them In the name of the Father, and of the Son, and of the Holy Ghost. Hear, we beseech thee, the prayer of thy Church; sanctify this water to the mystical washing away of sin; and grant, that *this child* now to be baptized therein, may receive the fulness of thy grace and ever remain in the number of thy faithful children; through Jesus Christ our Lord, to whom with thee and the Holy Spirit be all honour and glory, now and for evermore.

Answer: Amen.

THE BAPTISM

Then shall the Priest take the child into his arms, or by the hand, and shall say to the godfathers and godmothers:

Priest: Name this child.

And then naming the child after them, he shall dip it in the water, or pour water on it, saying:

Priest: N., I baptize thee in the name of the Father, and of the Son, and of the Holy Ghost. Amen.

THE RECEPTION

Priest: We receive *this child* into the congregation of Christ's flock, and do sign* *him* with the sign of the Cross in token that hereafter *he* shall not be ashamed to confess the faith of Christ crucified, and manfully to fight under

* Here shall the Priest make a Cross upon the child's forehead.

his banner against sin, the world, and the devil; and to continue Christ's faithful soldier and servant unto *his* life's end. Amen.

Then the Priest, still holding it in his arms, or by the hand, shall pronounce this blessing upon it, after which he shall give the child again to the godparents.

N., the Lord take thee into his holy household, clothe thee with the robe of innocency, write thy name in the book of life, and keep and govern thee evermore. *Amen.*

THE THANKSGIVING

Priest: Let us give thanks unto Almighty God, and with one accord make our prayer for *this child* in the words of our Saviour Christ, saying together,

Priest and People: Our Father, which art in heaven, Hallowed be thy name; Thy kingdom come; Thy will be done; in earth as it is in heaven. Give us this day our daily bread. And forgive us our trespasses, As we forgive them that trespass against us. And lead us not into temptation; but deliver us from evil: For thine is the kingdom, The power and the glory, For ever and ever. Amen.

Priest: We yield thee hearty thanks, O merciful Father, that it hath pleased thee to give *this infant* new birth by thine own Spirit;

Answer: We thank thee, O God.

Priest: And to receive *him* for thine own child;

Answer: We thank thee, O God.

Priest: And to graft *him* into the body of Christ's Church;

Answer: We thank thee, O God.

Priest: And to make *him* an inheritor of thine everlasting kingdom.

Answer: We thank thee, O God.

Priest: Praise ye the Lord;
Answer: The Lord's name be praised.

Then shall follow this prayer for the home:

Priest: Almighty God, our heavenly Father, whose blessed Son shared at Nazareth the life of an earthly home: Bless, we beseech thee, the home of *this child*; and inspire those who have the care of *him* with thy wisdom and continual help; through the same thy Son, Jesus Christ our Lord.
Answer: Amen.

Then he may dismiss the congregation with this blessing:

Priest: The blessing of God, the Father, the Son, and the Holy Spirit, rest upon you now and always. *Amen.*

CONFIRMATION

INTRODUCTORY NOTE

Confirmation is the focus of what the Church does for and with boys and girls. Therefore the steps that lead to it and that lead from it are of crucial importance and have to be related to the other influences and events in the life of the adolescent, such as going from school into industry and commerce.

Important also is it to give thought and care to the arrangements for the immediate preparation for the actual service, and the continuing preparations for First Communion. In the immediate preparation and in the ordering of the service,

(1) parents and godparents and the congregation have to be helped to realize that they are not there as spectators, but are taking part in a corporate act of the Church in which their thoughts and prayers are of its essence. Therefore it is desirable to put into their hands not only the order of service but some explanations and prayers. It is also important to make the members of the local Church realize that the Confirmation is an event in its life in which they have a part. The growing custom, admittedly not easy to maintain year after year, of a communicant member acting as a sponsor for a candidate, standing beside him or her when the Bishop confirms and holding a card on which the Christian name of the candidate is clearly printed for the

Bishop to see, is commendable: and it does not add appreciably to the length of the service if the procedure is carefully rehearsed.

(2) The candidates have to be helped to be unselfconscious, and to be both relaxed and receptive. A careful rehearsal is an aid to this and so are some preparatory prayers at the beginning of the service.

(3) At the outset, as far as may be, a pastoral relationship between Bishop and candidates has to be created. Fortunate is the Bishop who has the gift of making quick personal contacts without obtruding his personality unduly in the actual Confirmation. If one has not this gift it helps both Bishop and candidates if he says the preparatory prayers himself standing in the aisle among them. If he is already well known to them he may leave this to the incumbent and make his opening words a Salutation and the reading of the Preface. Alas, the prefaces as provided are a hindrance. The 1662 one has no pastoral or devotional value and is more suitable as a prefatory note on the service paper: the 1928 revision is open to theological criticism. Might not bishops be allowed to say what is required to be said informally, if they could resist the temptation to turn it into the first of two addresses?

From the Promises through to the end of the prayers after the Confirmation, no hymns should be interpolated.

The simple service in the Prayer Book is great in its simplicity and should not be smothered in hymns, least of all sentimental, subjective hymns. It then becomes clear to the dullest of adults what it signifies and it makes by its very reticence and concentration a strong emotional appeal, different from that of the First Communion and not to be confused with it.

Here follow instructions to incumbents, private prayers, and corporate preparatory devotion and suggestions in regard to hymns. With the help of Fr. Richard Roseveare, S.S.M., now Bishop of Accra, who was one of my incumbents in 1939, we prepared a service paper which included these and was available for every candidate and the congregations, and was in use with minor changes during an episcopate of over 22 years. To make clear how the preparation leads into the Order of Confirmation and the usage in regard to hymns, by permission the Order has been printed in part. I like the straightforward realistic words of commission before the blessing of the candidates as in 1928. In contrast to the sentimentality in which the rite has often been draped they express succinctly the quality of faith and life which enabled the Apostolic Church to be victorious over paganism and would enable the Church to be effectively militant today.

Instructions to Clergy in regard to the Service

The congregation should be told on previous Sundays, and the parents when they are visited, to be in their places at least ten minutes before the service is timed to begin. On arrival they should be asked to read, or there should be read to them, the note addressed to them in the printed Order (cf. infra).

When the candidates enter in procession the congregation should stand to receive them.

It is unhelpful to candidates if numbers of younger children are present who cannot keep quiet or be kept in order.

The candidates should be made thoroughly familiar with the service, with what they have to do and say, and helped to use well the time of waiting and silence. There should be a careful rehearsal a day or two before, at which all taking any active part should attend.

The candidates should be in their places five minutes before the service begins. There should be no coming and going of sidesmen and wardens during those minutes but the stillness of silent prayer. Any instructions or notices should be given at the outset of this period.

The candidates should all be seated *immediately* in front of the Bishop. No other persons—clerical or church officers—should sit in front of them. If any of the choristers are being confirmed they should sit with and be with the other confirmees throughout the service, and *not* with the Choir.

Ample seating-room should be allowed for the candidates, care should be taken to see it is easy for them to kneel, and that each is provided with the Order of Service (which they should be allowed to keep) and with a hymn book if it is being used.

The veils worn by female candidates should be simple and uniform, and properly put on. Uniformity is assured if the P.C.C. is possessed of a sufficient stock of veils and lends them to the candidates. White dresses are not essential and 'dressing up' is not desirable. Boys should be asked not to plaster their hair with sticky lotions!

When the Bishop confirms by name, a way to make this error-proof is that *each candidate should bring up a card with* the one Christian name by which he or she is usually called written in block capitals upon it. This they should give to the persons or person standing by the bishop who will hold it so that he can read the name easily. (The one name only is important for it is homely and friendly, whereas to use all the Christian names strikes a formal, not to say legal, note).

If the design of the church allows, the confirmees should kneel a little below the level on which the Bishop's chair is placed.

The candidates should come up to the Bishop quietly in a continuous stream. If there has been a rehearsal it is unnecessary that they should be marshalled, still less pushed around, by sidesmen.

When the seats are open at both ends they can come out at one end and return by the other. When they are not, all the occupants should come out into the aisle at one time and stand there so that those seated at the end farthest from the opening go up to the Bishop first and those nearest to the opening last.

Stepping over one another's feet, or sliding along the seats, is not conducive to private prayer. This should be carefully rehearsed. A rehearsal helps to make the candidates feel relaxed and unself-conscious.

The candidates should not be distracted by having to find a coin for the offertory. The service moves most smoothly when the collection is not 'taken up', but is received at the doors as the congregation leaves.

The 'Amen' at the end of 'Defend, O Lord, this thy child *N*.' is said by the Bishop alone. The other 'amens' in the service should be *said*, not sung. The service should end with the Blessing.

It is not helpful if the organist extemporizes or plays a tune on the organ during the administration of the Sacrament.

No hymn should be interpolated between the Promises and the prayers following the Confirmation.

THOUGHTS AND PRAYERS BEFORE THE SERVICE BEGINS

(a) *For candidates (before the service begins):*

This is a solemn moment in your life. You come in faith to be received into full membership of the Church of Christ, and to receive the Holy Spirit of God to keep you loyal and make you strong in his service.

Kneel down and try to be still in the Presence of God. Offer yourself to him in your own words, or in these:

O ever-loving God, who hast made me for thyself, I thank thee for having called me into thy family wherein I have learnt to know, love, and serve thee: Make ready my heart and will to renew the vows of my baptism and to receive thy Holy Spirit; that as a faithful soldier and servant I may follow thy blessed Son Jesus Christ unto my life's end. Amen.

Lord Jesus:

> Lead me that I may follow thee;
> hold me that I may hold me fast by thee;
> teach me that I may learn of thee;
> give me thy love that I may love thee. Amen.

Then sit, and read slowly these Scriptures:

Be strong and of good courage; fear not, nor be dismayed: for the Lord God, even my God, will be with thee; he will not fail thee, nor forsake thee.

From St. Mark's Gospel:

Now after that John was put in prison, Jesus came into

Galilee, preaching the gospel of God, and saying, The time is fulfilled, and the Kingdom of God is at hand: repent, and believe the gospel.

And as he walked by the sea of Galilee, he saw Simon and Andrew his brother casting a net into the sea: for they were fishers. And Jesus said unto them, Come with me, and I will make you to become fishers of men. And straightway they forsook their nets and followed him. And when he had gone a little farther thence, he saw James the son of Zebedee, and John his brother, who also were in the ship mending their nets. And straightway he called them: and they left their father Zebedee in the ship with the hired servants, and went after him.

From St. Paul's Epistles:
A description of the Church, and the source of its strength.

We, being many, are one body in Christ, and every one members one of another. As the body is one and has many members, and all the members of that body, being many, are one body; so also is Christ. For by one Spirit are we all baptized into one body. If one member suffer, all the members suffer with it: or if one member be honoured, all the members rejoice with it. Now you are the body of Christ and each of you members of it.

(b) *For parents, godparents and others present.*

The Bishop in confirming acts on behalf of the whole Church by authority of Christ conferred on him by the laying on of hands with prayer.

You represent the Church also, and especially the local congregation into whose fellowship and life the candidates are being received.

You are not spectators at this service. By your thoughts and prayers you will be co-operating with the Bishop. Only if you do this will what is done be all that God intends it to be for those about to be confirmed.

During the actual Confirmation the congregation are asked to kneel or sit as each may prefer, joining their thoughts and prayers with those of the candidates: reminding themselves of their own Confirmation and their Communions; or may be asking why they have never come forward for Confirmation and have not made more effort to accept the responsibilities of life in the light of God's purpose for the world as Jesus Christ declares it to be. Whatever your thoughts, pray for those now offering themselves to be followers of Jesus Christ and resolve both to come with them when they make their First Communion, and also to travel with them on the Way.

THE ORDER OF SERVICE

THE PREPARATION

HYMN (*after all have entered*)

[*All kneel*]

The Bishop, or a priest whom he may appoint, shall say:

Thou O Lord art in the midst of us and we are called by thy holy name.

We wait for thy loving-kindness, O God, in the midst of thy temple.

Thou shalt show us the path of life: in thy presence is the fullness of joy.

Let us call upon the Holy Spirit who cometh from the Father and the Son:

Look graciously upon us, O Holy Spirit, and grant us for our hallowing thoughts that pass into prayer, prayer that passes into love, and love that passes into life with thee for ever. *Amen.*

Let us pray to be delivered from wandering thoughts and be enabled to think of God and of the gift he is about to give.

Almighty God, unto whom all hearts be open, all desires known, and from whom no secrets are hid: Cleanse the thoughts of our hearts by the inspiration of thy Holy Spirit, that we may perfectly love thee, and worthily magnify thy holy name; through Christ our Lord. *Amen.*

Let us pray that we may grow in the knowledge of God.

O Almighty God, whom truly to know is everlasting life; grant us perfectly to know thy Son Jesus Christ to be the way, the truth, and the life; that, following the steps of thy holy Apostles, we may steadfastly walk in the way that leadeth to eternal life; through the same thy Son Jesus Christ our Lord. *Amen.*

Finally, that we may live and grow in the love of God, let us pray.

O Almighty and most merciful God, of thy bountiful goodness keep us, we beseech thee, from all things that may hurt us; that we, being ready both in body and soul, may cheerfully accomplish those things that thou wouldest have done; through Jesus Christ our Lord. *Amen.*

Then all shall say, still kneeling, with him:

> I bind unto myself today
>   The power of God to hold and lead,
> His eye to watch, his might to stay,
>   His ear to hearken to my need.
> The wisdom of my God to teach,
>   His hand to guide, his shield to ward;
> The word of God to give me speech,
>   His heavenly host to be my guard.

(from St. Patrick's Breastplate)

[All stand]

HYMN

THE PROMISES

The Bishop, having proceeded to his chair, shall say:

Grace to you and peace from God our Father and the Lord Jesus Christ.

And all shall answer firmly: Amen.

[Candidates remain standing. Congregation sits.]

One of the appointed Prefaces is read (or the Bishop himself may speak as suggested on pp. 100–1).

Then the Bishop shall say to those to be confirmed:

You, then, who are to be confirmed must now declare before this congregation that you are steadfastly purposed, with the help of this gift, to lead your life in the faith of Christ and in obedience to God's will and commandments; and must openly acknowledge yourselves bound to fulfil the Christian duties to which your Baptism has pledged you.

And the service shall continue as in the Book of Common Prayer.

THOUGHTS AND PRAYERS FOR CANDIDATES BEFORE AND AFTER THE LAYING ON OF HANDS

(a) *Before you go up.*

If you are not among the first to be confirmed, watch the Bishop confirming the first two, and then pray quietly in simple words of your own, such as these—repeating them perhaps several times:

Lord Jesus Christ, my Master and Friend, thou art calling me into thy service and company.

Holy Spirit of the Father and the Son, thou wilt make me unafraid and strong and keep me loyal.

God who created me, bless me and all who are being confirmed. Evermore. Amen.

Father of all; Jesus, Lord and King; Spirit of Love and Courage; Thine is the Kingdom, the Power and the Glory.

(b) *After you return.*

Kneel, and try to realize that the love and power of God is with you, about you, and in you. Repeat the words used by the Bishop as he laid his hand upon your head.

Thanks be to God for power to live as his sons and daughters.

Jesus, confirm my heart's desire
To think and work and speak for thee.

Praise the Lord, O my soul, and all that is within me praise his holy Name.

Take thou my thoughts
    that they may rest on thee,
Take thou my words
    that they may tell of thee,
Take thou my deeds
    that they may honour thee.

THE CONCLUSION OF THE SERVICE

When all have been confirmed,
[The congregation kneels, the newly-confirmed stand.]

Bishop: The Lord be with you;

Answer: And with thy spirit.

All together: Our Father . . . for ever and ever. Amen. [*The confirmed also kneel.*]

Bishop: Let us pray.

Almighty and ever-living God, who makest us both to will and to do those things that be good and acceptable unto thy Divine Majesty: We make our humble supplications unto thee for these thy servants, upon whom (after the example of thy holy apostles) we have now laid our hands, to certify them (by this sign) of thy favour and gracious goodness towards them. Let thy fatherly hand, we beseech thee, ever be over them; let thy Holy Spirit ever be with them; and so lead them in the knowledge and obedience of thy Word, that in the end they may obtain everlasting life; through our Lord Jesus Christ who with thee and the Holy Spirit liveth and reigneth, ever one God, world without end. *Amen.*

Then shall he bless the newly-confirmed:

Go forth into the world in peace; be of good courage; hold fast that which is good; render to no man evil for evil; strengthen the fainthearted; support the weak; help the afflicted; honour all men; love and serve the Lord, rejoicing in the power of the Holy Spirit.

And the blessing of God Almighty, the Father, the Son, and the Holy Spirit, be upon you, and remain with you for ever. *Amen.*

HYMN

THE BISHOP'S ADDRESS

HYMN

Bishop: Let us pray.

Then shall be said by all together with the Bishop:

O Almighty Lord, and everlasting God, vouchsafe, we beseech thee, to direct, sanctify, and govern both our hearts and bodies, in the ways of thy laws, and in the works of thy commandments; that, through thy most mighty protection both here and ever, we may be preserved in body and soul; through our Lord and Saviour Jesus Christ. *Amen.**

THE BLESSING

No hymn shall follow here, but all shall go out in order.

HYMNS AT CONFIRMATION

A Confirmation Service may lose its direct simplicity and be unduly prolonged if there are too many hymns, or hymns too subjective or sung to weak, sentimental tunes, and also if they are not closely related to the several parts of the service. From much use we commend:

Opening:

>Glorious things of thee are spoken . . .
>City of God, how broad and far . . .
>Christ is our corner-stone . . .
>Lift up your heads, ye gates of brass . . .

(*or if the Confirmation is on a Festival or in its Octave, one for that Festival*)

After Preparation:

>O thou who camest from above . . .
>Breathe on me, Breath of God . . .
>Come down, O Love divine . . .

*To use two prayers following the Lord's Prayer results in loss of attention. The second (a Prayer of Trust which also comes in the Marriage Service, 1928) is better as a concluding prayer, said corporately after a moment of silence before the Blessing.

After Confirmation:

> Jesus, good above all other . . .
> He who would valiant be . . .
> O God of truth whose living Word . . .
> Strong Captain, in thy holy ranks . . .
> Father, hear the prayer we offer . . .
> Fill thou my life, O Lord my God . . .

After the Address:

> Thy kingdom come! on bended knee . . .
> Ye servants of God, your Master proclaim . . .
> Jesus shall reign where'er the sun . . . (*with 'alleluia's.*)

Note. References to standard hymn books for words and recommended tunes will be found in the Index of Hymns, pages 198 ff.

ALTERNATIVE PREFACE

In place of one of the appointed prefaces (p. 96) the Bishop may speak after this sort:

In ministering Confirmation the Church follows the example of the Apostles and the teaching of Holy Scripture. The laying on of hands with prayer—the prayer of all of us—is an outward sign and pledge of an inward grace—the giving of the Holy Spirit to those who in Baptism were received into the family of Christ's Church.

St. Paul makes plain the nature of this gift from God where he writes,

> 'The fruit of the Spirit is love, joy, peace, long-suffering, kindness, goodness, faithfulness, gentleness, self-control.'

The gift will wither and decay unless, obedient to the will of God and disciplined like true soldiers, you put it to good use. So St. Paul writes in another letter,

'Put on the whole armour of God, that you may be able to withstand in an evil day, and having done all, to stand.'

and again,

'Be imitators of God and walk in love as Christ loved us and gave himself for us.'

And Jesus, our Lord, himself says,

'Greater love has no man than this, that a man lay down his life for his friends. You are my friends if you do what I command you. . . . You did not choose me but I chose you and appointed you that you should go and bear fruit and that your fruit should remain.'

A FORM FOR PRIVATE CONFESSION AND ABSOLUTION

(*The closing sentence of the first Exhortation in the 1662 Communion Service reads:*

'If there be any of you who . . . cannot quiet his own conscience but requireth further comfort and counsel let him come to me* or to some other discreet and learned Minister of God's Word, and open his grief: that by the ministry of God's holy Word he may receive the benefit of absolution together with *spiritual* counsel and advice, to the quieting of his conscience, and avoiding of all scruple and doubtfulness.')

At the time appointed the Penitent shall kneel down in some convenient place in the church, and after silence has been kept for a space the Priest shall say:

Let us pray.

Almighty God, unto whom all hearts be open, all desires known, and from whom no secrets are hid: Cleanse

* The parish priest; cf. the words used at the Ordination of a priest.

the thoughts of our hearts by the inspiration of thy Holy Spirit, that we may perfectly love thee and worthily magnify thy holy name: through Christ our Lord. *Amen.*

and then turning to the Penitent he shall say:

The Lord be with your heart and your lips that you may rightly and honestly confess your sins.

Then shall the Penitent make particular confession of his sins in some such form as this:

I confess to God Almighty, the Father, the Son, and the Holy Spirit, before the whole company of heaven and you, my father, that I have sinned in thought, word, and deed through my own grievous fault: wherefore I pray God to have mercy upon me.

And especially I have sinned in these ways . . . .

The confession ended, the Priest shall give such counsel and direction as he thinks fit and if he is satisfied that penitence is full and sincere he shall absolve the Penitent, saying:

Our Lord Jesus Christ who left power to his Church to absolve sinners who truly repent, of his great mercy forgive all that you have done wrong. By his authority committed unto us, I declare that you are absolved from all your sins, in the Name of the Father, and of the Son, and of the Holy Spirit. Amen.

or more simply to one who makes confession regularly,

The Almighty and merciful God grant you pardon and remission of all your sins, time for amendment of life, and the grace and comfort of the Holy Spirit. Amen.

After a pause he may conclude by saying the Collect for Easter,

and then bid the Penitent join in saying as a thanksgiving for
God's pardon and love the Lord's Prayer (in full).
And the Penitent may use, in silent prayer, this short thanks-
giving:

O God, I have received from thee the grace of a new
life; grant that this gift may be the source of my joy.

THE MINISTRY TO THE SICK

INTRODUCTORY NOTE

Those who are in good health, even when they are sym-
pathetic and imaginative, find it hard to realize how limited are
the powers of attention of those who are seriously ill. If a hospital
patient is also unaccustomed to reading then the putting of a
printed act of devotion in his hands, far from helping, may
distract him from focusing his attention on the Sacrament
itself. Time and again one has had to say to a seriously ill and
weak patient 'Put the card down: just relax and try to rest in the
Lord. I will tell you what to do or to say if necessary.'

Partly for this reason the devotions that follow are shorter
than some in circulation and there is more emphasis on silence.
A priest's ministry to a seriously ill person more often than not
is to bring him or her consciously into the presence of the
Shepherd of his soul and then to withdraw his own personality. One of the most saintly of men preferred an indifferent
nursing home when his last illness overtook him to a general
hospital because, so he said, the chaplain fussed around too
much and would not leave him alone—with God.

The Visitation of the Sick in the Prayer Book of 1662 is for
several reasons no longer usable. The revision and expansion
of it in 1928 with much material taken from 'the Grey Book' is a
valuable quarry for the visiting priest or minister. Commendable also are the forms of prayer and the counsel in the
booklet (in typescript) issued by the Guild of Health (26 Queen
Anne Street, London W.1) in revised form in 1961 for nine-
pence. S.P.C.K. publish forms: *The Administration of Holy
Unction and the Laying on of Hands*, approved by the Convocation of York in 1936. Pastoral experience since then,
however, suggests the need for more flexibility.

I. PREPARATION FOR HOLY COMMUNION, LAYING ON OF HANDS, ETC.

The aim is to win the patient's co-operation by leading him into the right attitude and frame of mind. The following passages from the Guild of Health booklet are to the point.

'God is the Spirit of Life revealed to us in Jesus Christ working always with the whole creation expressing His own wholeness. It is His will to heal us and He can be trusted. His will can be hindered by our own sin, by unbelief, and even by negative thoughts in our own deep mind or in the minds of those around us, as well as by the evil in the world.'

Therefore those ministering to a sick person must do their best to help him to overcome these hindrances:

(1) *By simple trust in God which surrenders self-concern even about physical healing if possible.*

(2) *By repentance and acceptance of God's forgiveness.*

(3) *By prayer and quiet meditation.*

II. THE LAYING ON OF HANDS

At the outset the priest or minister should try to get the patient to relax and trust in God's mercy and goodwill. He should also let him know that after the Blessing he will slip away as he wants the patient to remain quite relaxed believing as firmly as he can in the healing power of God working within him.

The priest or minister reads a verse from one of the familiar psalms of trust (Psalms 23, 91, 121).

SILENCE

The priest then shall say—(or in his own words):

The eternal life of God was in Christ Jesus who went

about doing good, healing the sick, bringing forgiveness and peace of mind to those troubled in conscience and anxious.

SILENCE

Jesus said: I have come that men may have life and have it in all its fullness. Abide in me and I in you. Without me you can do nothing.

SILENCE

Say after me:

'Lord Jesus, I would be alive with thy life'.

In the silence he repeats this slowly; and adds this prayer:

O Almighty God, who art the giver of life and health and the aid of them that look to thee for succour: we call upon thee to give strength by the laying on of hands to this thy servant: that being made whole and well *he* may give thanks unto thee in thy Holy Church: through Jesus Christ our Lord. Amen.

Then the priest lays hands on the head of the sick person saying:

Our Lord Jesus Christ, who gave authority and power to his disciples to lay hands on the sick that they might recover, have mercy upon you; and by the authority committed unto me in his Church I now lay hands upon you that you may be made whole through the power and in the Name of Jesus Christ.

SILENCE

A BLESSING

III. THE COMMUNION OF A SICK PERSON

Collect.

Almighty and Eternal God, giver of life and health, grant that by thy goodness and mercy to this thy servant and to those who minister to him he may be restored to health and may in the body of thy Church walk before thee humbly and faithfully all his days: through Jesus Christ our Lord. *Amen.*

Epistle: 2 Corinthians 1.3–5.

Gospel: St. John 5.24 *or* St. John 10.14–15, 27–30.

The Sacrament should normally be administered to sick persons in both kinds together by intinction, especially in hospitals. This should be explained to them beforehand.

IV. THE ANOINTING OF A SICK PERSON

This form should only be used after consultation with the patient's doctor and with the understanding and desire of the person to be anointed.

He should be prepared by teaching about faith, repentance, prayer, and grace, and about God's ways of healing through scientific knowledge and medical skill.

For the anointing, a small table covered with a cloth should be set nearby, and on it placed the vessel with the oil, and cotton wool on a saucer with which to wipe the patient's forehead and the priest's thumb. (It should be burnt afterwards.)

Oil is generally blessed by the Bishop beforehand— according to tradition this was done annually on Maundy Thursday. Or the priest may do it before the anointing. The vessel of Holy Oil should be kept in an aumbry in church.

There should be silence after the Blessing and the priest and others about him should leave the patient resting without further talking.

When all is set the priest shall say the antiphon. It is repeated at the end of the psalm.

O Saviour of the world who by thy Cross and Passion hast redeemed us: save us and help us, we humbly beseech thee, O Lord.

Psalm 23

[Then a short Lesson may be read—James 5.14–15.]

If the sick person has not already made confession and received absolution and he is fully conscious, the priest shall say:

Let us confess our sins to God—you saying after me: O God our Father I am sorry I have sinned so often and so much. Make me truly repentant. I ask thy forgiveness—and thy grace to enable me to live a better life; through Jesus Christ, my Lord and Saviour. Amen.

Priest: The Almighty and merciful Lord grant you pardon, absolution, and remission of all your sins; and the grace and comfort of the Holy Spirit. Amen.

The priest shall then say this prayer:

O Almighty God, who art the giver of all health and healing and the aid of them that look to thee for succour: we call upon thee to bring strength and renewal to this thy servant, that being made whole and well, *he* may give thanks unto thee in thy holy Church: through Jesus Christ our Lord. Amen.

The priest shall then dip his thumb in the Holy Oil and make the sign of the Cross on the person's forehead, saying:

N., in the faith of Jesus Christ I anoint thee with this holy Oil and in the Name of God, Father, Son, and Holy Spirit. Amen.

And laying his hand on the person's head he shall continue:

As with this oil your body is outwardly anointed, so may your whole being [or mind and heart] be sanctified by the Holy Spirit of God. May the merciful Father give you release from pain and disease and restore you to health; and may he also give you faith to offer your sufferings in communion with our crucified Lord as a prayer for others; through the same Jesus Christ, our Lord. Amen.

The priest may then say one of these sentences followed by silence and, if desired, a Blessing:

Jesus said, 'Abide in me and I in you'. 'I am come that they might have life.'

If the oil has not already been blessed by the Bishop the priest shall say this prayer before using it:

O Lord God, who hast taught us by thy holy Apostle St. James to anoint the sick with oil that they may regain health, bless and hallow this oil for this purpose, we beseech thee, that the person who shall be anointed may be delivered from all evil and distress of body and mind: through Jesus Christ our Lord. *Amen.*

OTHER PRAYERS AND COMMENDATIONS

For Healing

O God, who by the might of thy command canst drive away from men's bodies all sickness and infirmity; be present in thy goodness with this thy servant, that *his* weakness being banished, and *his* health restored, *he* may live to glorify thy holy Name; through our Lord Jesus Christ. *Amen.*

For a Sick Child

O Lord Jesus Christ, who didst with joy receive and bless the children brought to thee, give thy blessing to this thy child; in thine own time deliver *him* from *his* bodily pain, that *he* may live to serve thee all *his* days. *Amen.*

For a Dying Child

O Lord Jesu Christ, the only begotten Son of God, who for our sakes didst become a babe in Bethlehem; We commit this child unto thy loving care. Send thy holy angel to lead *him* gently to those heavenly habitations where the souls of them that fall asleep in thee have perpetual peace and joy, and fold *him* in the everlasting arms of thine unfailing love; Who livest and reignest with the Father and the Holy Spirit, one God, world without end. *Amen.*

For a Convalescent

Lord, whose compassions fail not, and whose mercies are new every morning; we give thee hearty thanks that it hath pleased thee to give to this our *brother* both relief from pain and hope of renewed health. Continue, we beseech thee, in *him* the good work that thou hast begun; that, daily increasing in bodily strength, and humbly rejoicing in thy goodness, *he* may so order *his* life as always to think and do such things as shall please thee; through Jesus Christ our Lord. *Amen.*

For One Troubled in Conscience

Blessed Lord, the Father of mercies and the God of all comfort; we beseech thee, look down in pity and compassion on thy servant, whose soul is full of trouble; give *him* a right understanding of *himself*, and also of thy will for *him*, that *he* may neither cast away *his* confidence in thee, nor place it anywhere but in thee; deliver *him* from the fear of evil; lift up the light of thy countenance upon *him*, and give *him* thy peace; through the merits and mediation of Jesus Christ our Lord. *Amen.*

A Commendation

Go forth upon thy journey from this world, O Christian soul, in the name of God the almighty Father who created thee, and of Jesus Christ who suffered for thee, and of the Holy Spirit who strengtheneth thee. *Amen.*

May thy portion this day be with all who rest in Christ, in a place of green pastures, and by waters of comfort, where grief and misery are banished, and refreshment, light, and peace for evermore abide. *Amen.*

For Those in Trouble

Father of all, whose presence is everywhere and whose mercy never faileth, graciously regard all who are in trouble or danger and especially those known to ourselves (whom we now name in our hearts before thee): guide the wanderer, defend the innocent, restore the lost, heal the sick, comfort the sorrowing, befriend the lonely, and receive the spirits of the dying; through Jesus Christ our Redeemer. *Amen.*

AN ORDER OF SERVICE FOR THE BURIAL OF THE DEAD

Which may be used in a Public Cemetery and Chapel or at a Crematorium when the Order in the Book of Common Prayer is felt to be unsuitable, the mourners consenting.

[All stand]

The Minister, going before the body into the Chapel, shall say one or more of these sentences:

Remember not the sins and offences of my youth; but according to thy mercy think thou upon me.

Man that is born of a woman is of few days and full of trouble.

We brought nothing into this world, and it is certain we can carry nothing out. The Lord gave, and the Lord has taken away; blessed be the name of the Lord.

The Eternal God is your refuge, and underneath are the everlasting arms.

Neither death, nor life, nor angels, nor principalities, nor powers, nor things present, nor things to come, nor height, nor depth, nor any other creature, shall be able to separate us from the love of God which is in Christ Jesus our Lord.

Then shall be said one or more of the following psalms, and before and at the end shall be said:

Minister and People together: O Saviour of the world who by thy Cross and Passion hast redeemed us; Save us and help us, we humbly beseech thee, O Lord.

Psalm 130

Minister: Out of the deep have I called unto thee, O Lord: Lord, hear my voice.

People: O let thine ears consider well: the voice of my complaint.

Minister: If thou, Lord, wilt be extreme to mark what is done amiss: O Lord, who may abide it?

People: For there is mercy with thee: therefore shalt thou be feared.

Minister: I look for the Lord; my soul doth wait for him: in his word is my trust.

People: My soul waits for the Lord: more than watchmen for the morning.

Minister: O Israel, trust in the Lord, for with the Lord there is mercy: and with him is plenteous redemption.

People: And he shall redeem Israel: from all his sins.

Psalm 121

Minister: I will lift up mine eyes unto the hills: from whence cometh my help.

People: My help cometh even from the Lord: who hath made heaven and earth.

Minister: He will not suffer thy foot to be moved: and he that keepeth thee will not sleep.

People: Behold, he that keepeth Israel: shall neither slumber nor sleep.

Minister: The Lord himself is thy keeper: the Lord is thy defence upon thy right hand;

People: So that the sun shall not smite thee by day: neither the moon by night.

Minister: The Lord shall preserve thee from all evil: yea, it is even he that shall keep thy soul.

People: The Lord shall preserve thy going out, and thy coming in: from this time forth for evermore.

Psalm 23

Minister: The Lord is my shepherd: therefore can I lack nothing.

People: He shall feed me in a green pasture: and lead me forth beside the waters of comfort.

Minister: He shall convert my soul: and bring me forth in the paths of righteousness, for his Name's sake.

People: Yea, though I walk through the valley of the shadow of death I will fear no evil: for thou art with me, thy rod and thy staff comfort me.

Minister: Thou shalt prepare a table before me against them that trouble me: thou hast anointed my head with oil, and my cup shall be full.

People: But thy loving-kindness and mercy shall follow me all the days of my life: and I will dwell in the house of the Lord for ever.

At the ending of the psalm or psalms shall be said again:

Minister and people together: O Saviour of the world, who by thy Cross and Passion hast redeemed us; Save us, and help us, we humbly beseech thee, O Lord.

[*All sit*]

THE LESSON

From 1 *Corinthians* 15*:*

But now hath Christ been raised from the dead, the first fruits of them that are asleep. For since by man came death, by man came also the resurrection of the dead. For as in Adam all die, so also in Christ shall all be made alive. But some one will say, How are the dead raised? and with what manner of body do they come? Thou foolish one, that which thou thyself sowest is not quickened, except it die: and that which thou sowest, thou sowest not the body that shall be, but a bare grain, it may chance of wheat, or of some other kind; but God giveth it a body even as it pleased him, and to each seed a body of its own. So also is the resurrection of the dead. It is sown in corruption; it is raised in incorruption: it is sown in dishonour; it is raised in glory: it is sown in weakness; it is raised in power: it is sown a natural body; it is raised a spiritual body. For this corruptible must put on incorruption, and this mortal must put on immortality. But when this corruptible shall have put on incorruption, and this mortal shall have put on immortality, then shall come to pass the saying that is written, Death is swallowed up in victory. O Death, where is thy victory? O Death, where is thy sting? The sting of death is sin. But thanks be to God, which giveth us the victory through our Lord Jesus Christ. Wherefore, my beloved brethren, be ye stedfast, unmoveable, always abounding in the work of the Lord, forasmuch as ye know that your labour is not in vain in the Lord.

Or, St. Matthew 5.3–10 and Revelation 14.13:

Blessed are the poor in spirit, for theirs is the kingdom of heaven. Blessed are those that mourn, for they shall be comforted. Blessed are the meek, for they shall inherit the earth. Blessed are those who hunger and thirst for righteousness, for they shall be satisfied. Blessed are the merciful, for they shall obtain mercy. Blessed are the pure in heart, for they shall see God. Blessed are the peacemakers, for they shall be called sons of God. Blessed are those who are persecuted for righteousness' sake, for theirs is the kingdom of heaven.

Blessed are the dead who die in the Lord; they rest from their labours, and their works follow them.

or

Hear what our Lord and Saviour Christ says:

My sheep hear my voice, and I know them, and they follow me; and I give unto them eternal life, and they shall never perish. My Father who has given them unto me is greater than all; and no one is able to snatch them out of the Father's hand.

Hear also what Saint Paul says:

To them that love God all things work together for good. For I reckon that the sufferings of this present time are not worthy to be compared with the glory that shall be revealed to us.

Our light affliction, which is but for a moment, is preparing for us a far more exceeding and eternal weight of glory; because we look not at the things which are seen, but at the things which are not seen; for the things which are seen are temporal, but the things which are not seen are eternal.

Hear also what Saint John says:

God shall wipe away all tears from their eyes; and there shall be no more death, neither sorrow, nor crying, neither shall there be any more pain; for the former things are passed away. And he that sat upon the throne said, Behold, I make all things new.

(*A hymn may be sung here and a short address given.*)

[*All kneel*]

THE PRAYERS

Minister and people together: Lord, have mercy upon us:

  Christ have mercy upon us:

  Lord, have mercy upon us:

Our Father which art in heaven, Hallowed be thy Name; Thy kingdom come; Thy will be done; In earth as it is in heaven. Give us this day our daily bread; And forgive us our trespasses, As we forgive them that trespass against us; And lead us not into temptation; But deliver us from evil. Amen.

Minister: Almighty God, the fountain of all wisdom, who knowest our necessities before we ask, and our ignorance in asking; We beseech thee to have compassion upon our infirmities; and those things, which for our unworthiness we dare not, and for our blindness we cannot ask, vouchsafe to give us, for the worthiness of thy Son Jesus Christ our Lord. *Amen.*

Minister: Enter not into judgement with thy servant, O Lord:

People: For in thy sight shall no man living be justified.

Minister: O God our heavenly Father, whose mercy never fails, be gracious, we pray thee, to this our *brother* departed; that being loosed from the bonds of mortality and of sin *he* may be perfected by thy grace and enter at the last with all thy faithful ones into life eternal; through Jesus Christ our Saviour and Lord. *Amen.*

Minister: Blessed are they that mourn;

People: For they shall be comforted.

Minister: Almighty God, Father of all mercies and giver of all comfort; Deal graciously, we pray thee, with those who mourn, that, casting every care on thee, they may know the consolation of thy love; through Jesus Christ our Lord. *Amen.*

Minister: O Lord, show thy mercy upon us;

People: And grant us thy salvation.

Minister: Almighty God, who hast given us grace at this time with one accord to make our common supplications unto thee; and dost promise, that when two or three are gathered together in thy name thou wilt grant their requests: Fulfil now, O Lord, the desires and petitions of thy servants, as may be most expedient for them; granting us in this world knowledge of thy truth, and in the world to come life everlasting. *Amen.*

The grace of our Lord Jesus Christ, and the love of God, and the fellowship of the Holy Spirit, be with us all evermore. *Amen.*

[*All stand*]   (*Another hymn may here be sung.*)

THE COMMITTAL

On the way to the grave or in the Chapel if it be a cremation, the Minister may say one or more of these sentences:

Like as a father pitieth his own children: even so is the Lord merciful unto them that fear him.

For he knoweth whereof we are made; he remembereth that we are but dust. The days of man are but as grass; for he flourisheth as a flower of the field. For as soon as the wind goeth over it, it is gone; and the place thereof shall know it no more.

But the merciful goodness of the Lord endureth for ever and ever upon them that fear him: and his righteousness upon children's children.

Jesus said, I am the Resurrection and the Life. He who believes in me, though he die, yet shall he live. Whoever lives and believes in me shall never die.

We commend unto thy hands of mercy, most merciful Father, our *brother* departed, and commit *his* body* to the ground; earth to earth, ashes to ashes, dust to dust. And we beseech thee of thy infinite goodness to give us grace to live in thy fear and love, that in the day of judgement both this our *brother* and we may be found acceptable in thy sight; through him who died and liveth to make intercession for us, even Jesus Christ our Lord. *Amen.*

Thereafter the Minister shall give this blessing:

Unto God's gracious mercy and protection we commit our departed *brother*, *his* home and family, and all of you: the Lord bless you and keep you, and give you peace now and evermore. *Amen.*

At a cremation this prayer may be said before the Blessing:

O Heavenly Father, who in thy Son Jesus Christ hast

---

* *At a cremation:* to be consumed; ashes to ashes . . .

given us a true faith, and a sure hope: Help us, we pray thee, to live as those who believe and trust in the Communion of Saints, the forgiveness of sins, and the resurrection to life everlasting, and strengthen this faith and hope in us all the days of our life: through the love of thy Son, Jesus Christ our Saviour. *Amen.*

NOTE
If the people should not have the Order of Service in their hands, then instead of the versicles the Minister should say 'Let us pray for . . .'

AN OUTLINE OF A MEMORIAL SERVICE

All standing, the Minister shall say:

Let us commend to the mercy of God his servant . . . with our prayers, our thanksgiving, and our love.

THE WORDS OF FAITH AND TRUST

The Minister shall say:

Blessed be God, even the Father of our Lord Jesus Christ.

So God loved the world that he gave his only-begotten Son, to the end that all that believe in him should not perish but have eternal life.

Blessed are they that walk in the law of the Lord, and seek him with their whole heart.

To them that love God all things work together for good.

Blessed are they that die in the Lord; they rest from their labours and their works do follow them.

His servants shall serve him, and they shall see his face.

The Lord gave and the Lord hath taken away. Blessed be the Name of the Lord.

THE PSALMS

At the beginning and again at the end this antiphon shall be said or sung, by all together:

> Rest eternal grant unto them, O Lord:
> And let light perpetual shine upon them.

From Psalm 15, 23, 121, 130, *two should be chosen, or Psalm* 103.

The antiphons could be different for each psalm, for example:

Ps. 15: 'Rest eternal', *as above.*

Ps. 23: 'Though I walk through the valley of the shadow of death: I will fear no evil.'

Ps. 121: 'My help cometh even from the Lord: Who hath made heaven and earth.'

Ps. 130: 'If thou, Lord, wilt be extreme to mark what is done amiss: O Lord, who may abide it?'

PS. 103: 'The Lord hath prepared his seat in heaven: And his Kingdom ruleth over all.'

THE LESSON

Selected from Ecclus. 44.1–15; *Wisd.* 3.1–9; *Isa.* 54.7–8, 10; 1 *Cor.* 15.20 ff. (*See pp.* 113–14 *for a shortened version*); *Rev.* 21.22–27.

HYMN

(*Such as one of the following*):

> Happy are they, they that love God . . .
> The God of Love my Shepherd is . . .
> The Lord's my Shepherd, I'll not want . . .
> O God of Bethel, by whose hand. . . .

THE MEMORIAL ADDRESS

PRAYERS OF COMMENDATION

V. Blessed are the dead who die in the Lord:
R. They rest from their labours.

O Almighty Lord, the God of the spirits of all flesh, fulfil, we beseech thee, the purpose of thy love in those who are now at rest, that the good work which thou didst begin in them may be perfected unto the day of Jesus Christ, who lives and reigns with thee and the Holy Spirit, one God, world without end. *Amen.*

V. Blessed are they that mourn:
R. For they shall be comforted.

Almighty God, Father of all mercies and giver of all comfort: Deal graciously, we pray thee, with those who mourn, that casting every care on thee, they may know the consolation of thy love; through Jesus Christ our Lord. *Amen.*

For the continuing of the work to which *A.B.* gave the service of *his* life, let us pray.

V. He looked for the City which hath the foundations:
R. Whose builder and maker is God.

O God, thou art the source of all wisdom, goodness, and love, and without thine aid we can do no good thing: Continue thy blessing upon the undertaking in which our friend spent *him*self and upon the people for whom *he* cared; and grant, we beseech thee, that the sciences, arts, and industries may be ordered according to thy righteous will for the benefit of all peoples, through Jesus Christ our Lord. *Amen.*

Finally, a prayer for ourselves.

V. Thy loving kindness and mercy shall follow me:
R. All the days of my life.

Collect for Trinity IV or Trinity VI, and ending with the Ascription said by all together:

Now unto the King, eternal, immortal, invisible, the only wise God, be honour and glory for ever and ever. Amen.

[Then these words from the Russian Contakion for the departed may be sung:

Give rest, O Christ, to thy servant with the Saints:
Where sorrow and pain are no more: neither sighing, but life everlasting.

or the first verse of the carol This joyful Eastertide.

BLESSING

THE DEPOSITING OF ASHES AFTER CREMATION IN A GRAVE OR COLUMBARIUM

When the relatives are assembled the Minister shall say:

The souls of the righteous are in the hand of God, and no torment shall touch them. In the eyes of the foolish they seem to have died, and their journeying away from us to be their ruin, but they are in peace and their hope is full of immortality.

Then all shall say together Psalm 103.13–17:

Like as a father pitieth his own children: even so is the Lord merciful unto them that fear him.

For he knoweth whereof we are made: he remembereth that we are but dust.

The days of man are but as grass: for he flourisheth as a flower of the field.

For as soon as the wind goeth over it it is gone: and the place thereof shall know it no more.

But the merciful goodness of the Lord endureth for ever and ever upon them that fear him: and his righteousness upon children's children.

Glory be to the Father, and to the Son: and to the Holy Ghost;

As it was in the beginning, is now, and ever shall be: world without end. Amen.

As the Ashes are being placed the Minister shall say:

O God our Father, from whom we come and unto whom all souls return, forasmuch as it hath pleased thee in thy infinite wisdom and goodness to take unto thyself the soul of *A.B.*, we commit *his* mortal remains to their last resting-place in the faith that *he* is at rest with thee and in the sure hope of the resurrection to eternal life; through Jesus Christ who was dead and behold, is alive for evermore, and hath the keys of the grave and of death. *Amen.*

O Eternal Lord God, who holdest all souls in life: We beseech thee to shed forth upon thy whole Church in Paradise and on earth the bright beams of thy light and heavenly comfort; and grant that we, following the good example of those who have loved and served thee here and are now at rest, may at the last enter with them into the fullness of thine unending joy; through Jesus Christ our Lord. *Amen.*

And all shall join with him in saying the Lord's Prayer and the Grace:

Our Father, which art in heaven, Hallowed be thy name; Thy kingdom come; Thy will be done; In earth as it is in heaven. Give us this day our daily bread. And forgive us our trespasses, As we forgive them that trespass against us. And lead us not into temptation; but deliver us from evil; For thine is the Kingdom, The power, and the glory, For ever and ever. Amen.

The grace of our Lord Jesus Christ, and the love of God, and the fellowship of the Holy Spirit, be with us all evermore. Amen.

NOTE
At funerals, especially in crematoria and cemetery chapels, and at memorial services, effort should be made to get the congregation, including the mourners, to take an audible part in the service. Therefore it is desirable to put a full and clearly printed Order of Service into their hands.

IV

SPECIAL OCCASIONS

A DEVOTION ON A DIOCESAN OCCASION

'One Lord, One Faith, One Baptism,
One God and Father of all.'

———————

[All seated]

The Bishop will read words of our Lord declaring:
  —the truth in Jesus Christ:

This is life eternal, that they may know thee, the only
true God, and Jesus Christ whom thou hast sent.

—our unity in him:

They that are of the truth shall hear my voice. And
there shall be one flock, one Shepherd.

—our commission from him:

Jesus prayed—that they may all be one; as thou,
Father, art in me, and I in thee, that they may be one
in us; that the world may know that thou hast sent
me.

Alleluia. Amen.

Bishop: Let us stand and sing:

[All stand]

> Thy hand, O God, has guided
>   Thy flock, from age to age;
> The wondrous tale is written,
>   Full clear, on every page.

Our fathers owned thy goodness,
And we their deeds record;
And both of this bear witness,
'One Church, one Faith, one Lord.'

Bishop: Still standing, let us profess the Faith of the Church:

THE APOSTLES' CREED

And affirm the Mind and Charity of our Lord, saying:

THE BEATITUDES

V. Blessed are the poor in spirit;
R. For theirs is the Kingdom of heaven.

V. Blessed are they that mourn;
R. For they shall be comforted.

V. Blessed are the meek;
R. For they shall inherit the earth.

V. Blessed are they that hunger and thirst after righteousness;
R. For they shall be filled.

V. Blessed are the merciful;
R. For they shall obtain mercy.

V. Blessed are the pure in heart;
R. For they shall see God.

V. Blessed are the peacemakers;
R. For they shall be called the children of God.

V. Blessed are they which are persecuted for righteousness sake;
R. For theirs is the Kingdom of heaven.

(*pause*)

D.S.B.–K

V. Blessed are the dead who die in the Lord, saith the
Spirit;

R. For they rest from their labours and their works do
follow them.

OUR FATHER

Bishop: Peace be with you;

R.   And with thy spirit.

Bishop: In the Name of God, Father, Son, and Holy
Spirit. *Amen.*

THE BISHOP'S ADDRESS

HYMN

O Jesu, King most wonderful,
  Thou conqueror renowned,
Thou sweetness most ineffable,
  In whom all joys are found!

When once thou visitest the heart,
  Then truth begins to shine;
Then earthly vanities depart;
  Then kindles love divine.

O Jesus, light of all below,
  Thou fount of life and fire,
Surpassing all the joys we know,
  And all we can desire:

May every heart confess thy name,
  And ever thee adore;
And, seeking thee, itself inflame
  To seek thee more and more.

> Thee may our tongues for ever bless,
> Thee may we love alone;
> And ever in our lives express
> The image of thine own.

Bishop: The Lord be with you;
R. And with thy spirit.

[*All kneel*]

PRAYERS

including this Prayer for the Diocese:

Holy Father, Almighty and Everlasting God, who hast in the fullness of time through thy Eternal Son reconciled mankind unto thyself, and after his glorious Resurrection and Ascension didst manifest through his holy Church thy love and righteous will towards all men: Let thy Holy Spirit descend with sevenfold power upon the Bishop, clergy, and people of this diocese. Enable us to worship that men may know and adore the beauty of thy holiness; to live and labour that we may declare the greatness of thy love; to learn and teach that we may be faithful stewards of thy truth. And grant that, encompassed by those who are now in felicity, and strengthened by the fullness of thy power, we may enter into the joy of thy dear Son, to whom, with thee and the Holy Spirit, we ascribe honour, praise, and dominion now and evermore. *Amen.*

The prayers shall end with this Ascription said together:

Unto him who is able to do exceeding abundantly above all that we ask or think, according to the power that works in us; unto him be glory in the Church by Christ Jesus throughout all ages, world without end. *Amen.*

HYMN

Ye servants of God, your Master proclaim,
And publish abroad his wonderful name:
The name all-victorious of Jesus extol:
His kingdom is glorious, and rules over all.

God ruleth on high, almighty to save;
And still he is nigh; his presence we have.
The great congregation his triumph shall sing,
Ascribing salvation to Jesus our King.

Salvation to God, who sits on the throne!
Let all cry aloud, and honour the Son:
The praises of Jesus the angels proclaim,
Fall down on their faces, and worship the Lamb.

Then let us adore, and give him his right:
All glory and power, all wisdom and might,
All honour and blessing, with angels above,
And thanks never-ceasing, and infinite love.

Bishop: Still standing, let us say together:

THE GENERAL THANKSGIVING
[*All kneel*]

THE BLESSING

AN ACT OF DEDICATION

For a newly-elected Parish Church Council or a Diocesan Council:

A HYMN

A READING
from 1 *Corinthians* 1 (*New English Bible*)

SILENT MEDITATION

PRAYERS

Incumbent or Minister:

Let us ask God to cleanse us from unbelief and sloth and to forgive our failures to follow Jesus our Lord boldly and in all charity.

Collect for Trinity XXIV

Let us pray that in our work together, the Holy Spirit may guide our minds, kindle our hearts, confirm our wills.

Collect for Trinity IX

Let us pray that we may walk in the way which he has ✗ prepared for us to walk in.

O Lord Jesus Christ who art the Way, the Truth, and the Life, suffer us not to stray from thee who art the way, nor distrust thee who art the truth, nor rest in any other than thee who art the life; Teach us what to do, what to believe, and wherein to take our rest: we ask it for the glory of thy Name. *Amen.*

And now let us stand: and dedicate ourselves and the work we shall have to do in the coming year, saying together:

All: O Lord God, we acknowledge thee as our Father:
    ourselves as thy children:
    our neighbours as our brethren:
    And we dedicate to thy obedience:
    and to their service:
    our hearts and minds, our wills and works:
    Resolved to stand fast in thy faith:
    to seek the help of thy Holy Spirit:
    and to do battle for thy perfect Kingdom:
    In the Name of Jesus Christ our Lord. Amen. page 56

THE BLESSING

Then shall all sing:

> Praise God, from whom all blessings flow;
> Praise him, all creatures here below;
> Praise him above ye heavenly host;
> Praise Father, Son, and Holy Ghost. Amen.

A DIOCESAN FESTIVAL SERVICE

When all have passed in procession to their places, silence shall be kept for a space. Then the choir shall sing unaccompanied

THE SALUTATION

And plen-teous-ness with-in thy pa - - - - - la - ces.

boy I was glad.

* Adapted from the Motet 'Sacerdotes Domini' by William Byrd, by William Ellis, Mus. Doc. Master of the Music, Newcastle Cathedral, 1918-1938.

And the people will respond:

> O enter then his gates with praise,
>   Approach with joy his courts unto:
> Praise, laud, and bless his Name always,
>   For it is seemly so to do.

> For why, the Lord our God is good:
>   His mercy is for ever sure;
> His truth at all times firmly stood,
>   And shall from age to age endure.

If there is no choir or cantor the service will begin with the foregoing hymn in full:

> All people that on earth do dwell.

THE PREPARATION

The Minister shall say:

O come let us worship and fall down; for the Lord our God is holy;

And the people shall answer:

The Lord our God is holy.

Then shall all kneel and the Minister shall say:

O Lord God, our Creator, Saviour, and Strength, who hast made it thy highest glory to come down to the lowest part of our need; turn our souls, we beseech thee, to that constant beholding and full worship of thee, which shall abase them in their own sight and exalt them in thine, O Father, Son, and Holy Spirit, blessed for evermore. *Amen.*

Holy, righteous, and merciful God; that we may now offer thee true worship and joyful service, cleanse our minds and free our consciences from the things that hide thee from us, and grant us evermore the help of thy grace; through Jesus Christ our Redeemer and Lord. *Amen.*

> *V.* On our blindness to thy glory and forgetfulness of thy truth;
> *R.* Lord, have mercy.
>
> *V.* On our unwillingness to be led by thy Spirit;
> *R.* Lord, have mercy.
>
> *V.* On our failures in love and on our pride;
> *R.* Lord, have mercy.
>
> *V.* And from all denials of thee in daily life;
> *R.* Good Lord, deliver us.

Then shall the Bishop (or a Priest) pronounce this Absolution:

Almighty God, our heavenly Father, who of his great mercy hath promised forgiveness of sins to all them that with hearty repentance and true faith turn unto him: have mercy upon you; pardon and deliver you from all your sins: confirm and strengthen you in all goodness; and bring you to everlasting life; through Jesus Christ our Lord. *Amen.*

THE PRAISES

The Minister shall say:

For the pardon and joy that is ours in Christ Jesus, let us give thanks unto God, saying together:

Our Father, . . . for ever and ever. *Amen.*

Then all shall stand:

V. Glory be to the Father, and to the Son, and to the Holy Ghost;

R. As it was in the beginning, is now, and ever shall be, world without end. *Amen.*

The following hymn (or hymns) may be sung in procession. It should in that case be preceded by the words, Let us go forth in peace, *and the response,* In the Name of the Lord, *and an appropriate Collect should be said between the hymns and at the entry into the Choir,*

Jesus shall reign where'er the sun . . .

or Ye holy Angels bright . . .

Praise my soul, the King of heaven . . .

Praise to the Lord, the Almighty . . .

For all the Saints . . .

THE READING

One of the following passages, or a part thereof, shall be read:

St. Luke 14.12–35; St. John 12.20–32; St. John 15.1–11; St. John 1.1–18; Acts 4.5–13, 23–35; 1 Cor. 12.1–27; Eph. 3; Eph. 4.1–13; Col. 3.1–17; Rev. 5.

Then shall be sung:

Help us to help each other, Lord . . .

THE SERMON

(*A hymn may be inserted here if the preacher is not reading the prayers.*)

THE PRAYERS

(*Other intercessions or biddings may be added after the prayer for the diocese and before the prayer of dedication.*)

Jesus said: And I, if I be lifted up, will draw all men unto me.

For the Diocese

Holy Father, Almighty and Everlasting God, who hast in the fullness of time through thy Eternal Son reconciled mankind unto thyself, and after his glorious Resurrection and Ascension didst manifest through his holy Church thy love and righteous will towards all men: Let thy Holy Spirit descend with seven-fold power upon the Bishop, clergy, and people of this diocese. Enable us to worship that men may know and adore the beauty of thy holiness; to live and labour that we may declare the greatness of thy love; and to learn and teach that we may be faithful stewards of thy truth. And grant that, encompassed by those who are now in felicity, and strengthened by the fullness of thy power, we may enter into the joy of thy dear Son, to whom, with thee and the Holy Spirit, we ascribe honour, praise, and dominion now and evermore. *Amen.*

For the Dedication of Ourselves

O thou who wilt come to take account of thy servants, and judge us according to our works, have mercy upon us, who have known thy will but failed to do our part; cleanse us from unbelief and sloth, and fill us with hope and zeal, that we may do thy work and bear thy Cross and bide thy time and see thy glory, who livest and reignest with the

Father and the Holy Spirit, one God, world without end. *Amen.*

The grace of our Lord Jesus Christ, and the love of God, and the fellowship of the Holy Spirit be with us all evermore. *Amen.*

THE OFFERING

On occasions where there is not a special Offering and a collection is made in the customary way at this point, a longer hymn should be substituted. Otherwise may be sung:

The Church of God a kingdom is . . .

Parochial gifts shall then be presented by representatives to the Bishop seated in his chair and individual gifts shall at the same time be collected in the customary way. While the Offering is being made a short anthem may be sung.

The Offering having been presented and the people having knelt down, the prayers following shall be said:

O Lord God, we beseech thee of thy mercy to accept these offerings that we make, not of our own but of thine, for all things come of thee. And grant that gifts that can never be worthy of thy acceptance may yet be hallowed by thy blessing and used in thy service; through Jesus Christ our Lord. *Amen.*

V. Father, hallowed be thy Name;

R. Amen. Hallowed be thy Name.

V. Hallowed be thy Name in this [*or* our] Cathedral Church;

R. Amen.

V. Hallowed be thy Name in the churches and parishes of the diocese;

R. Amen.

V. Hallowed be thy Name in the life and work of its
towns and villages;

R. Amen.

V. Thine, O Lord, is the Kingdom, the Power, and the
Glory;

R. For ever and ever. Amen.

THE THANKSGIVING

Then all standing up, and the priests in the Sanctuary gather-
ing about the Holy Table, the Bishop, standing in the midst,
shall say:

Blessed be thou, O God our Father, for ever and ever.
Thine, O Lord, is the greatness and the power and the
majesty. All that is in the heaven and in the earth is thine.
In thy hand it is to make great and to give strength to the
children of men. Blessed be thy Name this day for the
founders and benefactors of this (Cathedral Church and)
Diocese; for the Saints and Martyrs who have lifted high
the Cross in our land; for evangelists and pastors who have
proclaimed the Gospel, and for all men and women of glad
and humble heart who have obeyed thy Word: Wherefore
in thanksgiving would we sing:

TE DEUM LAUDAMUS

[*If* Te Deum *is sung by a choir to an anthem setting, then*
shall follow the doxology, sung by all together.

> Praise God, from whom all blessings flow;
> Praise him, all creatures here below;
> Praise him above, ye heavenly host;
> Praise Father, Son, and Holy Ghost.]

Silence

THE BLESSING

There shall be no hymn or further prayers after the Blessing,
but the clergy and choristers shall leave the Church in their
order.

A SERVICE OF PRAISE FOR CHOIRBOYS OR YOUNG PEOPLE

The order is based on *Te Deum Laudamus* and was first used on 9 December 1933, at a choirboys' service in Newcastle Cathedral.

The organ shall play a cheerful voluntary at the entrance and a quiet interlude between the parts of the service.

The verses of the processional hymns shall be sung alternately by the processing choirs and those who keep their places.

[*All stand*]

All shall kneel down and in silence remember God's presence.

Reader: O God, make speed to save us;
Boys: O Lord, make haste to help us.
Reader: Grant, we beseech, thee, merciful Lord, to thy faithful people pardon and peace, that they may be cleansed from all their sins, and serve thee with a quiet mind; through Jesus Christ our Lord. *Amen.*
Reader: O Lord, open thou our lips;
Boys: And our mouth shall show forth thy praise.
Reader: Bless us, O Lord, with a vision of thy being and thy beauty: that in the strength of it we may do our part in thy service gladly and well. *Amen.*

[*All stand*]

Reader: Glory be to the Father, and to the Son, and to the Holy Ghost;
Boys: As it was in the beginning, is now, and ever shall be, world without end. Amen.
Reader: Praise ye the Lord;
Boys: The Lord's name be praised.

Then shall be sung :

> Worship, honour, glory, blessing,
>   Lord, we offer to thy name;
> Young and old, thy praise expressing,
>   Join their Saviour to proclaim.
> As the Saints in heaven adore thee,
>   We would bow before thy throne,
> As thy Angels serve before thee,
>   So on earth thy will be done.

Then follows an Explanatory Address.

THE WORSHIP OF GOD THE CREATOR AND FATHER OF ALL

[All stand]

Reader : We praise thee, O God:

Boys : We acknowledge thee to be the Lord.

Reader : All the earth doth worship thee:

Boys : The Father everlasting.

Reader : To thee all angels cry aloud:

Boys : The heavens and all the powers therein.

Reader : To thee Cherubim and Seraphim continually do cry:

Boys : Holy, holy, holy, Lord God of Sabaoth.

All : Heaven and earth are full of the majesty of thy glory.

Then shall be sung three verses of the hymn

> Praise to the Lord, the Almighty.

[All kneel]

Reader : Let us join together to thank God for all the good things that he has made and has given us to enjoy.

The General Thanksgiving (to be said by all)

THE WORSHIP OF JESUS CHRIST, OUR SAVIOUR

[*All stand*]

Reader: Thou art the King of Glory, O Christ:
Boys: Thou art the everlasting Son of the Father.
Reader: When thou tookest upon thee to deliver man:
Boys: Thou didst not abhor the Virgin's womb.
Reader: When thou hadst overcome the sharpness of
death:
Boys: Thou didst open the Kingdom of Heaven to all
believers.
Reader: Thou sittest at the right hand of God:
Boys: In the glory of the Father.

A Lesson (St. John 1.1–14)

Hymn
Jesus shall reign where'er the sun

THE WORSHIP OF THE HOLY SPIRIT IN CHURCH

[*All stand*]

Reader: O Lord, save thy people:
Boys: And bless thine inheritance.
Reader: Day by day we magnify thee:
Boys: And we worship thy Name ever world without
end.

A Lesson (Acts 4.5–13)

[*All kneel*]

Reader: For the churches to which we belong:
For their unity in the service and worship of
Jesus Christ:
For our homes and schools and for all whom we
love:

Let us say together:

Our Father . . .

Hymn
Pray that Jerusalem may have

THE PRAISE OF THE SAINTS IN HEAVEN

[*All stand*]

Reader: The glorious company of the Apostles:
Boys: Praise thee.
Reader: The goodly fellowship of the Prophets:
Boys: Praise thee.
Reader: The noble army of Martyrs:
Boys: Praise thee.
Reader: The holy Church throughout all the world
Boys: Doth acknowledge thee.
All: The Father, of an infinite Majesty:
         Thine honourable, true, and only Son:
         Also the Holy Ghost, the Comforter.

A Lesson (St. Matthew 25.31–40)

Thereafter all shall kneel, and the Dean or Provost, standing before the Holy Table, shall make a Commemoration of the Patron Saint and Founders of this [Cathedral] Church.

The Procession

For all the saints who from their labours rest

A station shall be made at the Rood.

Provost: We pray thee help thy servants, whom thou hast
         redeemed with thy precious blood:
Boys: Make them to be numbered with thy Saints in
         glory everlasting.

Collect for the Festival of the Patron Saint

Hymn
Jesus, good above all other

AN ACT OF DEDICATION

[*All kneel*]

Reader: Let us ask God to bless and defend us and to use us in his service.

Silence

Reader: O Lord, have mercy upon us:
Boys: Have mercy upon us.
Reader: O Lord, let thy mercy lighten upon us:
Boys: As our trust is in thee.
All: Defend us, O Lord, with thy heavenly grace, that we may continue thine for ever, and daily increase in thy Holy Spirit more and more until we come unto thine everlasting Kingdom. Amen.

Silence

Reader: O Lord, in thee have I trusted;
Boys: Let me never be confounded.

THE BLESSING

Go forth into the world in peace; be of good courage; hold fast that which is good; render to no man evil for evil; strengthen the faint-hearted; support the weak; help the afflicted; love all men; serve the Lord rejoicing in the power of the Spirit.

And the blessing of God Almighty, the Father, the Son, and the Holy Spirit, be with you always. *Amen.*

If a hymn be required for the going out on account of the number of choristers let it be a triumphant march like Ye servants of God, your Master proclaim.

D.S.B.–L

A FAMILY SERVICE ON
CHRISTMAS EVE

CEREMONY OF THE LIGHTING OF THE TREE

When it is dusk, children with their gifts and parcels for children who are homeless, orphans, or in hospital, together with their parents and others, seat themselves in front seats of the Nave.

The lights are turned down.

A server enters and lights the candles on the Altar.

The Priest says:

'I was a stranger and ye took me in.'

'The people that walked in darkness have seen a great light.'

Then voices unseen, or gathered round the Crib, sing:

Fairest Lord Jesus,
Lord of all creation,
　Jesus, of God and Mary the Son;
Thee will I cherish,
Thee will I honour,
　O thou my soul's delight and crown.

Fair are the meadows,
Fairer still the woodlands,
　Robed in the verdure and bloom of spring.
Jesus is fairer,
Jesus is purer,
　He makes the saddest heart to sing.

Fair are the flowers,
Fairer still the sons of men,
　In all the freshness of youth arrayed:

> Yet is their beauty
> Fading and fleeting;
>> My Jesus, thine will never fade.

As the singing ends, the Priest of the Church walks down from the Sanctuary and taking one of the children by the hand leads him or her up to the Altar. There, turning to the people, he says:

The Lord is our light and our salvation: of whom then shall we be afraid?

And the people respond:

Show the light of thy countenance, O God; and we shall be whole.

Then, guided by the priest, the child lights a long taper from the altar candle, and together they walk down to the tree. The child lights a candle on the tree and, as he does so, all the lights on the tree are lit. The child says:

God is light: and in him is no darkness at all.

THE BRINGING OF GIFTS

Everyone joins in singing the carol:

> In the bleak mid-winter
>> Frosty wind made moan;
> Earth stood hard as iron,
>> Water like a stone;
> Snow had fallen, snow on snow,
>> Snow on snow,
> In the bleak mid-winter,
>> Long ago.

> Our God, heaven cannot hold him,
>> Nor earth sustain.
> Heaven and earth shall flee away
>> When he comes to reign:

In the bleak mid-winter
  A stable-place sufficed
The Lord God Almighty,
  Jesus Christ.

Angels and Archangels
  May have gathered there,
Cherubim and Seraphim
  Thronged the air:
But only his Mother,
  In her maiden bliss,
Worshipped the Beloved
  With a kiss.

What can I give him,
  Poor as I am?
If I were a shepherd
  I would bring a lamb;
If I were a wise man
  I would do my part;
Yet what I can I give him—
  Give my heart.

*Thereafter the children come and lay their presents at the foot
of the tree. And while they are standing about the tree the
Priest says the following prayers, first saying:* Inasmuch
as you have done it unto the least of these you have done
it unto me.

O God whose heart is as the heart of a child, hear our
prayer for children who are suffering through the sin,
hatred, and stupidity of men and women. In thy mercy
restore to them what has been taken from them. Raise up
fathers to the fatherless, mothers to the motherless, friends
to the friendless. Wipe out from their souls the stain of
misery and fear: and give back to them the trustfulness and

untroubled joy which should be theirs. To those who look after them and teach them, grant faith that thou art able to do this, and patient wisdom to co-operate with thee, for the sake of Jesus Christ who, taking the children in his arms, blessed them, saying, 'Of such is the kingdom of heaven.' *Amen.*

O Father of all who hast made known thy love to men by the birth of the holy Child at Bethlehem: help us to welcome him in our homes and to make room for him in our lives so that we may care for one another and live at peace with all thy family, through the same thy Son, Jesus Christ. *Amen.*

O God who hast made this holy night to shine with the illumination of the true light: grant we beseech thee, that we who have known the gladness of that light on earth may enjoy it perfectly in heaven: through the same our Lord and Saviour Jesus Christ. *Amen.*

THE BLESSING

A CAROL SERVICE DURING THE CHRISTMAS SEASON OR FOR THE EPIPHANY

This service was first arranged for the evening of Epiphany but it may be sung on the evening of Christmas or on any evening during the Christmas Season.

The ceremonial and music rubricks are designed for a Cathedral and some modifications will be required to suit the needs of smaller churches. The ceremonial is not essential to the service; the sequence of readings, carols, and hymns can be simply followed in a mission hall or a school classroom.

The Christmas Gospel should be read by the Dean or Incumbent, the other readings by various people, e.g., boys and girls of a school. In one Cathedral those who read were, in order, a bell-ringer, a choir-man, a deaconess, a chorister, a churchwarden, a canon.

The effect of the opening carol should be of a distant, unseen choir suddenly breaking in on the night air. It should therefore be un-announced and unaccompanied, and sung lightly and quickly—the organ entering at the end and continuing until the procession is in place. In a small church this effect may best be obtained by singing in the vestry or outside the porch or at the back of a west gallery. Similarly the closing carol should be sung unaccompanied by an unseen choir.

A Christmas Tree. A large tree is a lovely thing in a church. It adds greatly to the colourfulness of this service.

Gospeller's Procession. Two servers with candles and torches, canon or priest carrying gospel-book, Dean or Incumbent (in cope if worn), two servers with candles or torches, Cross-bearer.

Entry of Choir. During the singing of *Adeste Fideles* clergy and choir move to their places and the Gospeller's procession goes to the Sanctuary. A lectern should then be set at the entry to the Chancel and moved after the last reading.

––––––––––

The lights in the Church are turned down and those on the tree lit. A carol is sung in the Lady Chapel or from some place where the singers are hidden from the congregation, who remain seated.

Unto us is born a Son,
King of Quires supernal;
See on earth his life begun,
Of lords the Lord eternal.

Of this love and mercy mild
This the Christmas story:
And O that Mary's gentle child
Might lead us up to glory!

O and A and A and O,
Cum cantibus in choro,
Let our merry organ go,
Benedicamus Dom'no.

The words 15th century (trans. *G. R. Woodward*): the melody in
Piae Cantiones 1582.

A Gospeller's Procession moves from the Sanctuary to the crossing outside the chancel screen; the congregation stands as it approaches.

THE READING OF THE GOSPEL FOR CHRISTMAS DAY

The Gospel ended, the lights in the Church shall be turned up and the candles lit, and as clergy and choir enter all shall sing:

O come, all ye faithful.

During the singing the choir shall move to their places.

Thereafter the people shall kneel and the priest, standing before the Holy Table of the Sanctuary, shall say the Christmas Collect, and then all shall join in the General Thanksgiving.

THE SECOND READING

St. Luke 1.26–33, 38

[The congregation sits]

Then shall be sung Magnificat (Bridges in G).

[The congregation stands]

THE THIRD READING

Isaiah 9.2–7

[The congregation sits]

Then shall be sung, Benedictus to a familiar chant, and the hymn following.

[The congregation stands]

O little town of Bethlehem.

THE FOURTH READING

St. Luke 2.1–7

[The congregation seated]

Then the choir only shall sing this carol:

In dulci jubilo
Now sing we all io;
　He, my love, my wonder,
Li'th in presepio,
　Like any sunbeam, yonder
Matris in gremio
Alpha es et O.

O Jesu parvule
I yearn for thee alway:
　Listen to my ditty,
O puer optime,
　Have pity on me, pity:
O princeps glorie,
Trahe me post te.

O Patris caritas,
O Nati lenitas;
　All with us was over
Per nostra crimina:
　But then thou didst recover
Cœlorum gaudia:
O that we were there!

Ubi sunt gaudia
If that they be not there?
　Angels there are singing,
Nova cantica.
　Sweet bells the while a-ringing
In regis curia:
O that we were there!

Then all shall kneel and prayer be made—for the homeless and hungry; for homes and children.

The Family Prayer: Our Father . . .

Thereafter this hymn shall be sung, all standing:

Fairest Lord Jesus (*see page* 142)

[*All sit*]

ORGAN INTERLUDE

During or after this an offering may be made for the homeless, the hungry, or children who have lost their parents.

THE FIFTH READING
St. Luke 2.8–16

[*The congregation sits*]

Then shall the choir only sing the carol:

In the bleak mid-winter

After which all shall stand and sing:
Hark! the herald Angels sing

THE SIXTH READING
St. Matthew 2.1–12

[*The congregation sits*]

The reading ended, the choir shall sing this carol:

How far is it to Bethlehem?
Not very far.
Shall we find the stable-room
Lit by a star?

Can we see the little child,
Is he within?
If we lift the wooden latch
May we go in?

May we stroke the creatures there,
    Ox, ass, or sheep?
May we peep like them and see
    Jesus asleep?

If we touch his tiny hand
    Will he awake?
Will he know we've come so far
    Just for his sake?

Great kings have precious gifts,
    And we have nought,
Little smiles and little tears
    Are all we brought.

For all weary children
    Mary must weep,
Here, on his bed of straw
    Sleep, children, sleep.

God in his mother's arms,
    Babes in the byre,
Sleep, as they sleep who find
    Their heart's desire.

*Then all shall stand and join in this, which may be sung
in procession around the Church:*

Angels, from the realms of glory

THE SEVENTH READING
Romans 8.28, 31–end

[*The congregation sits*]

Thereafter all shall kneel and prayer be made:

For peace and for Christ's reign.

The Collect for St. Stephen or for the Epiphany.

The Ascription.

THE BLESSING

THE GOING FORTH

As the Clergy and Choir proceed out there shall be sung the hymn:

As with gladness men of old

Thereafter the congregation shall kneel and the lights be dimmed.

Minister: The Lord be with you;
Choir: And with thy spirit.
Minister: Let us bless the Lord;
Choir: Thanks be to God.

Then a small unseen choir shall sing this carol and, during the singing, the lights about the Holy Table shall be put out.

> *Lully, lulla, thou little tiny child,*
> *By by, lully lullay.*

O sisters too,
How may we do
  For to preserve this day
This poor youngling,
For whom we do sing,
  By by, lully lullay.

Herod the King,
In his raging
  Charged he hath this day
His men of might,
In his own sight
  All young children to slay.

That woe is me,
Poor child for thee!
    And every morn and day.
For thy parting
Neither say nor sing
    By by, lully lullay!

Minister: Let us depart in peace;

Choir: In the Name of the Lord. Amen.

Silence for a space.

PROCESSION AND EUCHARIST ON PALM SUNDAY

The Procession on Palm Sunday evokes our Lord's entry into Jerusalem which he made deliberately Messianic in its character (Matt. 21.5; Zech. 9.9; Isa. 62.11). It is also in itself symbolic of the passage from death to life: the progress of the People of God behind Christ, the Victor, to the Kingdom and City of God, represented by the church which the procession is going to enter. There is an old tradition in the Church, which probably grew out of Matt. 21.15–16, that our Lord was greeted and accompanied by young folk. The Procession, therefore, might well be made an opportunity to bring in a procession of youth (14–18 years). They should carry, not dried palm branches, but as those who took part in the first procession did, branches of trees with their buds (and flowers) on them formed and breaking into life after the death of winter.

Where possible the Procession should be from one church to another church. Where this is not possible it should be round the outside of the church re-entering by the main doorway. The Liturgical colour for the Procession is red.

I. THE BLESSING OF PALMS AND OF BRANCHES IN BUD

(*In the first church*)

(*If the custom of a church is to bless and distribute palms it should be done at this point.*)

The priest standing before the table on which the palms to be blessed and distributed are laid shall say:

Priest: In the name of God, Father, Son, and Holy Spirit, Amen.

The Lord be with you;

Answer: And with thy spirit.

Let us pray.

Priest and People: Our Father, which art in heaven, Hallowed be thy Name. Thy kingdom come. Thy will be done, in earth as it is in heaven. Give us this day our daily bread. And forgive us our trespasses, As we forgive them that trespass against us. And lead us not into temptation; But deliver us from evil: For thine is the kingdom, The power, and the glory, For ever and ever. Amen.

Priest: Bless, O Lord, these (branches of) palms, that during the year they may be a memorial to those who keep them of thy Cross and of thy victory over sin and death. *Amen.*

2. THE PREPARATION

Psalm 24

said or sung with this refrain or antiphon before and after:

Hosanna in the highest:
The Hebrew children sang.

Thereafter the procession of youth (pueri Hebraeorum) carrying branches in bud and flowers, shall form in the aisle, and they and all present shall stand facing the altar while the Priest reads the narrative of the Procession from the Mount of Olives into Jerusalem.

St. Matthew 21.1–9

People: Thanks be to God.

Priest: Let us go forth in peace;

Answer: In the name of the Lord.

Then the procession leaves the church led by a crucifer bearing the Processional Cross (unveiled) and by wardens carrying palms: making a station on the way, where the Collect for Palm Sunday is said:

Almighty and everlasting God, who, of thy tender love towards mankind, hast sent thy Son, our Saviour Jesus Christ, to take upon him our flesh, and to suffer death upon the cross, that all mankind should follow the example of his great humility; Mercifully grant, that we may both follow the example of his patience, and also be made partakers of his resurrection; through the same Jesus Christ our Lord. *Amen.*

As the procession of youth approaches the second church, its choir, grouped outside the main doorway, sings verses of St. Theodulph's hymn:

All glory, laud, and honour

and the Procession responds by singing the refrain:

All glory, laud, and honour
To thee, Redeemer, King,
To whom the lips of children
Made sweet hosannas ring.

3. IN THE SECOND CHURCH

The Procession, having entered, halts in the aisle before the Sanctuary.

A Reader shall read: St. Matthew. 21.10–16

And all shall respond: Alleluia. Thanks be to God.

Then shall be sung the hymn:

O Jesu, King most wonderful.

being the second part of Jesus, the very thought of thee (*12th century*).

Thereafter all pass to their places and the Celebrant begins the Holy Communion.

When there has not been a Procession, the Liturgy begins with the Kyrie and Collects.

The following preparation might be said before the Holy Communion.

[*All stand*]

Psalm 22.1–5

THE SENTENCES OF THE DAY

He came unto his own and they received him not.

He made himself obedient unto death, even the death of the Cross.

Silence

V. O Saviour of the world who by thy Cross and Passion hast redeemed us:

R. Save us and help us we humbly beseech thee, O Lord.

Psalm 22.19–26

This, the greatest of the Passion psalms, is precious to Christians because our Lord's thought rested upon it as he hung upon the Cross. It falls into three parts and the middle section is recited more appropriately on Good Friday.

[*All sit*]

OLD TESTAMENT LESSON

Isaiah 52.13–53.12

HYMN FOR INTROIT

Ride on, ride on in majesty.

COLLECT OF THE DAY

EPISTLE

Philippians 2.5–11

GRADUAL OR MEDITATION

Unto thee, O Lord, will I lift up my soul; my God, I have put my trust in thee: O let me not be confounded, neither let mine enemies triumph over me.

For all they that hope in thee shall not be ashamed: but such as transgress without a cause shall be put to confusion.

Show me thy ways, O Lord: and teach me thy paths.

Lead me forth in thy truth, and learn me: for thou art the God of my salvation; in thee hath been my hope all the day long. (Ps. 25.1–4).

While we were yet sinners, Christ died for us. Amen.

THE GOSPEL

Being the reading of the Passion

St. Matthew 26.1 (or 26.36)–27.61

or

St. Mark 14.1 (or 14.26)–15.41

The congregation to remain seated until Matt. 27.31 or Mark 15.21.

It may be possible in some churches to divide the reading among five persons

✠ Jesus
N. Narrator
D. Disciples and Friends
C. The Crowd
A. Adversaries.

The Creed is omitted.

OFFERTORY PSALM 22.18–32

(if not said already) or

HYMN

It is a thing most wonderful

or

O sacred head, sore wounded.

If the Passion has been read at one celebration, at others the Gospel may be St. Matthew 20.1–13.

DEVOTIONS FOR THE EVENINGS IN HOLY WEEK BEFORE GOOD FRIDAY

The *Liturgy* during this week

(1) recalls as fully and as clearly as possible the events and words of the last days of our Lord's earthly life and ministry;

(2) enables the Christian to enter into the mystery of God's redeeming work, emphasizing the part in it of baptism, penitence, and communion;

(3) makes him look forward both in humility and confidence to the life of which the Cross and Resurrection are the promise and the road.

This it does by the recital of psalms and the readings from the Scriptures at all the services. These are in sequence from service to service and day to day. To enable more people, especially in urban areas, to join in this daily reading and meditation, a group of churches might arrange some variety of use among themselves year by year, e.g., one might follow what is set out in the Book of Common Prayer fully; another, instead of reading all four narratives of the Passion, might concentrate more intensively on one. Again, Holy Communion might be celebrated after the working day is over, especially if a rule of a three-hour fast is kept. The reading of the Gospel might be made into a guided meditation, the congregation being seated.

Here follows an outline for Evening Communion on the first three days of the week, at which the Passion according to St. Mark is read and used as a guided meditation. Another year the Passion in one of the other Gospels might be read similarly.

For Maundy Thursday an order is also given and on that evening the Liturgy should be fuller and more colourful.

The *Order of Service* every evening:

Kneel down in silence.

Sentence of the Day spoken slowly and followed by silence.

Opening responses from Evensong.

Psalm. On the first three evenings the psalm is the Introit.

D.S.B.–M

A DEVOTION FOR THE WEEK

which may be used privately or said before the Blessing

O Lord Christ, Son of God, Lord of Lords,
call us, who are called to be saints,
    along the way of the Cross:
draw us, who would draw nearer our King,
    to the foot of thy Cross:
cleanse us, who are not worthy to approach,
    with the pardon of thy Cross:
arm us for the battles of holiness,
    by the might of thy Cross:
bring us, in the fellowship of thy sufferings,
    to the victory of thy Cross:
and seat us in the Kingdom of thy glory
    among the servants of thy Cross,
        O crucified Lord:
who with the Father and the Holy Spirit
    livest and reignest one God,
        almighty, eternal
        world without end.

(*A Procession of Passion Prayers.*)

MONDAY

Sentence of the Day

Is it nothing to you, all ye that pass by? Behold and see
if there be any sorrow like unto my sorrow.

Psalm 25

This great psalm has been the consolation of martyrs and saints. In
1685 one Covenanting lass, tied to a stake to await drowning in the
rising tide of the Solway, sang it with her last breath before the water
filled her lungs. It was on the lips of the dying St. Francois de Sales,
sixty years before.

Additional Collect

Almighty God, whose most dear Son went not up to joy but first he suffered pain and entered not into glory before he was crucified; Mercifully grant that we, walking in the way of the Cross, may find it none other than the way of life and peace; through the same thy Son, Jesus Christ our Lord. *Amen.*

For the Epistle
Jeremiah 11.18–20

The prophet Jeremiah, in his love for the people of God, in his persecution and rejection by them, and in his anguish of spirit, is a prototype of the Messiah's ministry and rejection. This is the lection for this day in the Roman Proper, which comes from early times. It is extraordinary that there should be no lesson from Jeremiah in the Book of Common Prayer or in any of our authorized lectionaries during the Lenten season.

Meditation

O go not from me for trouble is at hand: and there is none to help me.

Jesus comes unto his disciples and finds them asleep, and says, 'What could you not watch with me one hour?'

Meditation and Reading of the Gospel

On the successive evenings, the Gospel might be read by five readers

✠ Jesus
N. Narrator
D. Disciples and Friends
C. The Crowd
A. Adversaries.

It should be read, all being seated. The leader of the meditation, who should be 'the narrator', will interrupt the reading as he thinks well to make comment or to allow for meditation in silence.

St. Mark 14

Then may follow Intercessions (the Prayer for the Church Militant) or the Priest may proceed directly to the Invitation 'Ye that do truly and earnestly repent'.

TUESDAY

Sentence of the Day

Like as a father pitieth his own children: even so is the Lord merciful unto them that fear him.

Psalm 27

This Psalm is quoted in the pages written by the tortured Savonarola just before his end. Lady Jane Grey threw its words of courage to her husband before their execution as traitors. It consoled James Harrington, one of the martyrs of our own Church, in Central Africa in 1885.

Additional Collects

O Lord God, our heavenly Father, regard, we beseech thee, with thy divine pity the pains of thy children: and grant that the Passion of our Lord and his infinite love may make fruitful for good the trials of the innocent, the sufferings of the sick, and the sorrows of the bereaved: through him who suffered in our flesh and died for our sake; the same thy Son our Saviour Jesus Christ. *Amen.*

Jesus, Master, Carpenter, who at the last through wood and nails didst purchase man's whole salvation, wield well thy tools upon our lives that we who come to thee rough-hewn may by thy hand be fashioned to a truer beauty for thy glory's sake. *Amen.*

For the Epistle
Isaiah 42.1–7

This is the first of the four 'Suffering Servant' passages which are embedded in the second part of the Book of Isaiah. The poet probably was thinking of the vocation of Israel, the people of God, in the world. The Apostolic Church, and maybe our Lord himself, applied them to his vocation as Messiah and Saviour.

Meditation

Yea, though I walk through the valley of the shadow of death I will fear no ill.

(Jesus said:) 'Father forgive them for they know not what they do.'

The Gospel

(to be read as on Monday)

St. Mark 15.1–20

After a period of silence a Hymn about the Cross might be sung; thereafter the celebrant proceeds to the Invitation to confession.

WEDNESDAY

Sentences of the Day

And he said unto them, This is my blood of the new covenant, which is shed for many.

We love him because he first loved us.

Psalm 31.1–8, 18–end (B.C.P.)

This psalm reflects the thought and experience of Jeremiah, his passionate faith, his misery surrounded by hostility (vv. 9–17), and then the outburst of praise and confidence which makes so sudden a transition (v. 21ff.). It is a psalm which has been dear to Christians of all epochs and is hallowed by our Lord's Word upon the Cross.

Additional Collect

O Lord Jesus Christ, Son of the living God, who didst devote thy life and thy death to our most plenteous redemption: Grant that what thou hast wrought for us may be also wrought in us: that, growing into thy likeness, we may serve and share thy redeeming work; who livest and reignest in the glory of the eternal Trinity now and evermore. *Amen.*

For the Epistle

Isaiah 49.1–6

Another of the Suffering Servant passages.

Meditation

Whosoever of you will be the chiefest will be servant of all.

For the Son of man came not to be ministered unto but to minister.   (*St. Mark* 11. 43–44.)

The Gospel

St. Mark 15.21 to end of chapter

To be read and meditated upon as before. When the meditation is ended, all shall stand and the priest shall read in the Gospel again of the Crucifixion, vv. 24–39.

Instead of the customary response all shall bow the head and say:

O Saviour of the world who by thy Cross and Passion hast redeemed us: Save us and help us, we beseech thee, O Lord.

And thereafter all having knelt down and silence being kept for a space, the Priest shall begin the confession:

Almighty God, Father of our Lord Jesus Christ,

and so proceed with the Liturgy from that place.

MAUNDY THURSDAY

'Take and eat'

This day is dominated by the remembrance of the last meal which our Lord had with his apostles. There are ancient precedents for the growing practice of celebrating the Eucharist in the evening, and at an hour when many are able to make their communion. It is not desirable to alter the normal manner of celebration to make it look like the Last Supper, except that where it can conveniently be done the celebrant should face the people across the Holy Table as was the custom in the ancient basilicas. It was also ancient liturgical custom to re-enact ceremonially our Lord's washing of the disciples' feet, to consecrate oil for anointing, and at the end of the day to strip the Holy Table of its coverings and to extinguish all the lights—the people silently leaving the church in darkness.

Sentence of the Day

(Jesus said:) I am the bread of life: he that cometh to me shall never hunger. Having loved his own Jesus loved them to the end.

Psalm 23

Old Testament Lesson

Exodus 16.2–15

This story is the prototype of the coming of the true Bread of life.

Magnificat or Gloria in Excelsis

Additional Collects

Washing of the feet.

Almighty God, who didst disclose the precedence of thy Kingdom when our Lord before the Last Supper with his disciples washed their feet: Put away from us all pride of place and possession, that serving one another as he did we may be counted worthy to enter into the joy of our Lord: who with thee and the Holy Spirit, art God, blessed for evermore. *Amen.*

The Last Supper.

O Lord who hast left us in a wonderful Sacrament a memorial of thy Cross and Passion, grant us so to venerate the sacred mysteries of thy Body and Blood that we may know within ourselves the fruit of thy redemption: who livest and reignest with the Father and the Holy Ghost, one God, world without end. *Amen.*

The Epistle

1 Cor. 11.20–32

This passage has a two-fold interest. It shows that thirty or so years after the Crucifixion the celebration of the, Lord's Supper had become well established. It makes clear of what sort our love should be as we draw near to the Table of the Lord.

Meditation

Jesus said unto them: Verily I say unto you, Moses gave you not that bread from heaven, but my Father giveth you the true bread from heaven. For the bread of God is he who cometh down from heaven and giveth life unto the world.

The Gospel

St. John 13.1–17

A brief Meditation or Address may follow here

Before the Blessing, in place of Gloria in Excelsis, *the first Collect for Good Friday may be said.*

FESTAL OPENINGS FOR MATTINS AND EVENSONG

I. ASCENSION DAY

While the people are still seated, a Choir shall sing:

Hosanna to the Son of David. Blessed is the King that cometh in the Name of the Lord. Hosanna, thou that sittest in the highest heavens. Hosanna in excelsis Deo.

To the music of Thomas Weelkes, 1576–1623.

The Salutation

[*All stand*]

Thereafter the Clergy and Choir will proceed to their places and the Bishop, facing the congregation, shall say:

Christ the Lord ascended into heaven.
O come let us adore him, Alleluia.

Choir: Hail thee, Festival Day; blest day that art hallowed for ever;
Day when our Lord ascends high in the heavens to reign.

Bishop: God hath highly exalted him and given him a name which is above every name.

Choir: Hail thee, Festival Day; blest day that art hallowed for ever;
Day when our Lord ascends high in the heavens to reign.

Bishop: That at the name of Jesus every knee should bow and every tongue confess that Jesus Christ is Lord, to the glory of God the Father.

Choir: Hail thee, Festival Day; blest day that art hallowed for ever;

All: Day when our Lord ascends high in the heavens to reign. Alleluia.

Bishop: Grant, we beseech thee, Almighty God, that like as we do believe thy only-begotten Son our Lord Jesus Christ to have ascended into the heavens; so we may also in heart and mind thither ascend, and with him continually dwell, who liveth and reigneth with thee and the Holy Ghost, one God, world without end. *Amen.*

Minister: O God, make speed to save us;

People: O Lord, make haste to help us.

Minister: Glory be to the Father, and to the Son, and to the Holy Ghost;

People: As it was in the beginning, is now, and ever shall be, world without end. Amen.

Minister: Praise ye the Lord;

People: The Lord's Name be praised.

2. WHITSUNDAY

The Salutation

Choir: Alleluia! Alleluia! Alleluia!
Hail thee, Festival Day! blest day that art hallowed for ever;
Day wherein God from heaven shone on the world with his grace.

Bishop: The Spirit of God filleth the whole world, O come let us adore him. Alleluia.

Choir: Hail thee, Festival Day! etc.

Bishop: The Love of God hath been shed abroad in our hearts through the Holy Spirit.

Choir: Hail thee, Festival Day! etc.

Bishop: May God in all things be glorified through Jesus Christ our Lord.   Amen.

[*All kneel*]

Let us pray.

Look graciously upon us, O Holy Spirit, and grant us for our hallowing thoughts that pass into prayer, prayer that passes into love, and love that passes into life with thee for ever. *Amen.*

Thereafter follows the Order of Holy Communion, beginning at the Collect for the Day, or of Morning or Evening Prayer beginning at O Lord, open thou our lips.

[This pattern can be used for an Introit and Salutation on the other Great Festivals.]

3. HARVEST FESTIVAL

Psalm of Entry: Psalm 24

All standing, the Minister shall say:

The earth is the Lord's and the fullness thereof.
Great is his power, and his wisdom is infinite.

V. O let the earth bless the Lord;

R. Yea, let it praise him, and magnify him for ever.

V. O ye children of men, bless ye the Lord;

R. Praise him and magnify him for ever.

The Minister:

We are come together to praise God for his goodness and mercy and to make thanksgiving for the blessings of summer and the fruits of autumn; wherefore let us bow down and worship him with gladness.

All having knelt in silence, the Minister shall say:

O Lord, open thou our lips;

R. And our mouth shall shew forth thy praise.

Minister and People say together the General Thanksgiving.

The Minister:

O God, set our hearts at liberty from the service of ourselves and let it be our meat and drink to do thy will; through Jesus Christ our Lord. *Amen.*

Then may be sung a Harvest hymn and one or more of the appointed Psalms shall follow.

Thereafter, the Order shall proceed as in Morning or Evening Prayer.

The following Psalms are appropriate:
>   *Psalm 65, 104, 121, 145, 147, 148, 150,*
>   *and*
>   *Benedicite Omnia Opera.*

AN OPENING FOR A CIVIC SERVICE AND A LESSON OR LESSONS AT THE SAME

OPENING OF THE SERVICE

All shall kneel and the Minister shall say:

> Come, let us worship and fall down; for the Lord our God is holy;

People: The Lord our God is holy.

Minister: His kingdom is an everlasting kingdom;

People: His dominion endureth throughout all ages.

Minister: The kingdom of God is righteousness and peace and joy in the Holy Spirit;

People: Let us follow after things which make for peace.

Then shall all say together:

O God, our Father, whose will is our peace, strengthen and sustain the common life of this City. Forgive our sins and negligences: exalt our purposes: purify our aims: free us from selfish desires; may we be of one mind and heart in thy service; through Jesus Christ our Lord. Amen.

The Minister:

Grant, we beseech thee, merciful Lord, to thy faithful people pardon and peace: that they may be cleansed from all their sins, and serve thee with a quiet mind; through Jesus Christ our Lord. *Amen.*

Then after a short silence he shall say:

For the pardon and joy that is ours, let us give thanks unto God.

Our Father . . .

THE LESSON

Hear what the Old Testament saith:

Wisdom hath builded her house, she hath hewn out her seven pillars:

She crieth at the gates, at the entry of the city, at the coming in at the doors.

Unto you, O men, I call; and my voice is to the sons of man.

Receive my instruction and not silver; and knowledge rather than choice gold. For wisdom is better than rubies, and all the things that may be desired are not to be compared to it.

The fear of the Lord is to hate evil, pride and arrogancy: the fear of the Lord is the beginning of wisdom and the knowledge of the holy is understanding.

(*Proverbs* 9.1; 8.3–4, 10–11; 8.13; 9.10.)

There was a little city, and few men within it; and there came a great king against it, and besieged it, and built great bulwarks against it.

Now there was found in it a poor wise man, and he by his wisdom delivered the city; yet no man remembered that same poor man;

Then said I, Wisdom is better than strength: nevertheless the poor man's wisdom is despised, and his words are not heard.

The words of wise men are heard in quiet more than the cry of him that ruleth among fools.

Wisdom is better than weapons of war: but one sinner destroyeth much good. (*Ecclesiastes* 9.14–18.)

Therefore thus saith the Lord, Let not the wise man glory in his wisdom, neither let the mighty man glory in his might, let not the rich man glory in his riches:

But let him that glorieth glory in this, that he understandeth and knoweth me, that I am the Lord which exercise loving-kindness, judgment, and righteousness, in the earth: for in these things I delight, saith the Lord.
(*Jeremiah* 9.23–24.)

Hear also the words of Jesus Christ our Lord to those that would follow him:

Ye are the light of the world. A city that is set on an hill cannot be hid. Let your light so shine before men, that they may see your good works and glorify your Father which is in heaven.

The light of the body is the eye: if therefore thine eye be single, thy whole body shall be full of light. But if thine eye be evil, thy whole body shall be full of darkness. If therefore the light that is in thee be darkness, how great is that darkness!

No man can serve two masters: for either he will hate the one and love the other: or else he will hold to the one and despise the other. Ye cannot serve God and mammon.

Not every one that saith unto me, Lord, Lord, shall enter into the kingdom of heaven; but he that doeth the will of my Father which is in heaven.
(*St. Matthew* 5.14, 16; 6.22–24; 7.21.)

Therefore whosoever heareth these sayings of mine, and doeth them, I will liken him unto a wise man, which built his house upon a rock: And the rain descended, and the floods came, and the winds blew, and beat upon that house, and it fell not: for it was founded upon a rock.

And every one that heareth these sayings of mine, and doeth them not, shall be likened unto a foolish man, which built his house upon the sand: and the rain descended, and the floods came, and the winds blew, and beat upon that house; and it fell: and great was the fall of it.

And it came to pass, when Jesus had ended these sayings, the people were astonished at his teaching.

For he taught them as one having authority.

(St. Matthew 7.24–29.)

(The passages could be read by five different voices.)

VESTRY PRAYERS

Vestry Prayers should be said for and with those who are in the vestry, with the aim of enabling them to do their part in the act of worship more fittingly. They should not be intended to announce to the congregation that the service is about to begin, or to provide a post-benediction vesper for the congregation. They should be said *in* the vestry and not at the back of the church or in a doorway. It is desirable that the form should often be varied and that extempore words should sometimes be used.

Before Service:

> *Minister:* Let us keep silence.
> *(Pause.)*
> In the Name of God, and to his glory.
>
> *Choir:* Amen.
> *(Here may follow a short collect or extempore prayer.)*

After Service:

> *Minister:* The Lord be with you;
> *Choir:* And with thy spirit.

Minister: Let us depart in peace;
Choir:　　In the Name of the Lord, Amen.

or

Minister: Let us bless the Lord;
Choir:　　Thanks be to God. Amen.

Or these before and after the Holy Communion:

Before:

> *V.* In the Name of the Father, and of the Son, and of the Holy Spirit;
>
> *R.* Amen.
>
> *V.* The Lord is in his temple;
>
> *R.* Let the whole earth stand in awe of him.
>
> *V.* O send out thy light and thy truth, that they may lead me;
>
> *R.* And bring me unto thy holy hill, and to thy dwelling.
>
> *V.* And that I may go unto the altar of God;
>
> *R.* Even unto the God of my joy and gladness.

Priest: Let us pray.

Forgive, O Lord, what has been wrong in our thoughts and actions since we last served thee here; help us now to think of thee and to know that in this Sacrament thou art present in our midst, giving us strength to be loyal to thee in our daily life.

> *V.* Lord, hear this our prayer;
>
> *R.* And save us and help us, we humbly beseech thee. Amen.

After:

Priest: Let us pray.

Remember, O Lord, what thou hast wrought in us and not what we deserve, and as thou hast called us to thy service make us worthy of our calling; through Jesus Christ our Lord.

R. Amen.

V. The Lord be with you;

R. And with thy spirit.

V. Let us bless the Lord;

R. Thanks be to God. Amen.

V

PRAYERS FOR CHURCH AND SOCIETY

(A) PRAYERS

1. PREPARATION FOR INTERCESSION

Jesus said: If you abide in my words then are you truly my disciples. You shall know the truth and the truth shall make you free. Whatsoever you ask the Father in my Name he will give it you.

Eternal God whose majesty is revealed in mercy; grant that as we draw near to thee thy truth may set us free from the bondage of our own thoughts and desires, and that as we abide in thee our prayers may be an instrument of thy righteous will: through Jesus Christ our Lord. *Amen.*

O Holy Spirit, spirit of prayer, spirit of the sons of God: move us and all thy Church to pray for the cause for which Christ lived and died and lives to plead in heaven. *Amen.*

Also the Collect for Trinity X.

2. FOR A MISSION OF TEACHING

O God of truth and charity, be pleased to use these days of teaching, learning, and discussion to furnish thy Church with men and women committed unto thee. Direct and bless, we beseech thee, what is said and done in thy name that it may have success beyond our endeavour; through our Lord and Saviour Jesus Christ. *Amen.*

Everliving God, Trinity in Unity, wonderful beyond our thoughts in thy majesty and mercy; help us to meditate upon the splendour of thy creation and the compassion of thy redeeming work, that our faith in thy Kingdom, our hope in thy promises, our love towards all men, may be renewed and enlarged: for thy Name's sake. *Amen.*

O Lord Jesus Christ who art the way, the truth, and the life, suffer us not to stray from thee who art the way, nor to distrust thee who art the truth, nor to rest in any other than thee who art the life. Teach us what to believe, what to do, and wherein to take our rest; we ask it for the glory of thy Name. *Amen.*

3. FOR THE MISSION OF THE CHURCH

O God who art the light of the minds that know thee and the joy of loving hearts; grant that the life of the Church may be so quickened, the wisdom of its leaders so pure, the lives of its members so winning, that the power of the Gospel may be known in all the world and thy love for ever adored: through Jesus Christ who with thee, O Father, and the Holy Spirit, lives and reigns, One God, world without end. *Amen.*

O thou, who wilt come to take account of thy servants and judge us according to our works; have mercy upon us who have known thy will but have failed to do our part: Cleanse us from unbelief and sloth, and fill us with hope and zeal; that we may do thy work, and bear thy Cross, and bide thy time, and see thy glory; who livest and reignest, with the Father and the Holy Spirit, one God, world without end. *Amen.*

(Jerusalem Chamber Fellowship of Prayer.)

Renew us, O Lord God, with the vision of thy being and thy beauty, that in the strength of it we may do thy work without haste and without sloth; to thy eternal glory through Jesus Christ our Lord. *Amen.*

O Lord, thy Church exultant in joy makes its offerings unto thee: as thou hast given us such gladness in Thy Son's Resurrection, grant that we may know the harvest of joy eternal, through the same thy Son, Jesus Christ our Lord. *Amen.*

4. THANKSGIVING FOR A MISSIONARY

Holy and Merciful Father, whose will it is that all men should be saved and come to the knowledge of the truth, we praise and thank thee for the witness of thy Church in all lands to which thy servant, our departed *brother*, *N.*, gave the service of *his* life: And grant, we beseech thee, that the work which in thy providence *he* began and continued may by thy Holy Spirit come to its fruition, through Jesus Christ our Lord. *Amen.*

5. COMMEMORATION OF FOUR SERVANTS OF GOD

Saint Francis of Assisi (4 Oct.)

O God most holy and pitiful, who didst kindle a flame of love in the heart of Saint Francis, so that it became wholly thine; Increase in us the same faith and power of love, that as we rejoice in his humility and victorious deeds we may know the secret of his perfect joy; through Jesus Christ our Lord. *Amen.*

(*Proper Epistle*, Philippians 2.1–11; *Gospel*, St. Luke 9.2–6; 46–48; *and before the Blessing the prayer he inspired*:)

Eternal God, Father of all men, we commit to thee the needs of the whole world; where there is hatred give love; where there is injury, pardon; where there is distrust, faith; where there is despair, hope; where there is darkness, light, for the sake of Jesus Christ our Lord. *Amen.*

Saint Martin of Tours (11 Nov.).

O Almighty God, who didst endue thy soldier, Saint Martin, with the spirit of courtesy and sacrifice and didst make him a bishop and apostle of the faith; grant us grace to grow in his likeness and, serving men, to glorify thee, and at the last to attain unto thy eternal Kingdom; through Jesus Christ our Lord. *Amen.*

(*Proper Epistle*, 1 Thessalonians 5.5–11; *Gospel*, St. Matthew 25.31–40.)

Saint Hugh of Lincoln (17 Nov.)

O merciful Father, who didst endow thy servant, Hugh, with a wise and cheerful boldness and enable him to rebuke king and princes and commend to them and all men the discipline of love; give us grace, like him, to be bold and to have just cause for boldness, even the fear and love of thyself alone; for t' e sake of Jesus Christ our Lord. *Amen.*

(*Lesson*, Ecclus. 45.2–4; *Gospel*, St. Matthew 24.42–47.)

A Commemoration of William Temple, Archbishop of Canterbury (b. 15 Oct., 1881; d. 26 Sept., 1944)

O God who art glorified in the perfect offering of thy Son and hast given through him the promise of thy Kingdom: grant that, thy truth illuminating our minds and thy love purifying our hearts, we may after the example of thy servant, William Temple, be generous and bold in the service of that Kingdom: through the same Jesus Christ our Lord. *Amen*

(*Lesson*, Jeremiah 9.23–24; *Gospel*, St. John 17.1–8.)

6. THE ECUMENICAL MOVEMENT AND REUNION. THE CHURCH OVERSEAS

Those who are responsible for the Week of Prayer for Christian Unity issue every year a leaflet of prayers.

A full order of service was prepared many years ago by the late Bishop Edward Woods for 'Friends of Reunion', who publish it.

Every year before St. Andrew's-tide prayers for the overseas life and mission of the Church are prepared and circulated to all incumbents in the Church of England.

In recent years many books of prayers, litanies, and thanksgiving have been compiled and published at the service of clergy and ministers, e.g.:

After the Third Collect, *by Dean Milner White* (*Mowbrays*).

The Kingdom, the Power, and the Glory (*O.U. Press*).

The material, old and new, out of which an individual priest can make his own selection, is now very extensive.

7. PRAYERS FOR A DIOCESE

Holy Father, Almighty and Everlasting God, who hast in the fullness of time through thy Eternal Son reconciled mankind unto thyself, and after his glorious Resurrection and Ascension didst manifest through his holy Church thy love and righteous will towards all men: Let thy Holy Spirit descend with sevenfold power upon the Bishop, clergy, and people of this diocese. Enable us to worship that men may know and adore the beauty of thy holiness; to live and labour that we may declare the greatness of thy love; to learn and teach that we may be faithful stewards of thy truth. And grant that, encompassed by those who are now in felicity, and strengthened by the fullness of thy power, we may enter into the joy of thy dear Son, to whom, with thee and the Holy Spirit, we ascribe honour, praise, and dominion now and evermore. *Amen.*

O God, who hast called us to be members together of thy Church, which is the Body of thy Son; pour out, we beseech thee, thy Spirit on this diocese. Endue with strength and love and wisdom all who bear authority therein. Accept our gifts, our labours, and our love, and use them for the advancement of thy Kingdom and the glory of thy Name. Lead us in all our work for thee, and unite us in the joyful service of thy Son, our Saviour Jesus Christ. *Amen.*

See also supra p. 175, '*The Mission of the Church*'.

A Prayer of a Congregation—for Choirboys

O Lord, who hast taught us to take thought for the well-being of all children, bless and protect our choristers and choirboys; and give to clergy and choirmasters and their elders in the church such sincerity of mind and discernment in love, that these boys (and girls) may never, through familiarity with sacred things, grow careless in their worship or unmindful of their loyalty to thee, but may grow up in thy holy Church and love to obey thee, who art their Saviour and Friend. *Amen.*

For a Church under Repair

O Lord God of our fathers, by whose guiding the people of . . . were led in days of old to build this Church, and by whose inspiration they were enabled to make it beautiful and good; help us to show our thankfulness in reverent care of their work. Guide and protect, we beseech thee, those who are now repairing it, that the building may be preserved for the generations that will follow us; to the praise and worship of thy glorious Name; through Jesus Christ our Lord. *Amen.*

8. FOR A TOWN

O God our Father, in whose will is our peace, strengthen and sustain the common life of this community: forgive our sins and negligences; exalt our purposes; purify our aims that we may be of one mind in thy service; through Jesus Christ our Lord. *Amen.*

O God who hast taught us to live in the cities of this world as knowing our citizenship to be in heaven; bless the people of . . . and guide with thy heavenly wisdom the Mayor, Aldermen, Councillors, and those who bear office in the same; that they may ever keep before their eyes the vision of that City which hath the foundations, whose Builder and Maker is God; through Jesus Christ our Lord. *Amen.*

Eternal God, whom truly to know is to love, and by whose Spirit men are led into the way of blessedness; grant that the people of this city may feel after thee and find thee; and, we beseech thee, hasten the coming day when, sin and disease being subdued, our homes may be beautiful and our common life healthful and glad; to the hallowing of thy holy Name; through Jesus Christ our Lord. *Amen.*

9. FOR THE HEALTH SERVICES AND HOSPITALS

O God our Father, as we praise thee for thy mercy and goodness through the past years so we beseech thee to continue thy work of healing among us; Grant to physicians, surgeons, nurses, and all who co-operate with them, wisdom and skill, patience, strength, and tenderness, that by their endeavour many may be made whole in body and mind; through Jesus Christ our Lord. *Amen.*

See also the Ministry to the Sick, pp. 103–110.

10. FOR SOCIAL SERVICES

Heavenly Father, thou hast given us thy dear Son to be our light and salvation: Grant us grace to reveal his brightness to others and to render it back to thee in our own lives: Prosper and protect this undertaking for the well-being of *thy children,* and let thy blessing be upon it: through the same Jesus Christ, to whom be praise and glory evermore. *Amen.*

Almighty God, from whom to be turned is to fall, to whom to be turned is to rise, and in whom to abide is to stand: grant us in all our duties thy help; in our perplexities thy guidance; in dangers thy protection; in our sorrows thy comfort; and in our happiness thy hallowing spirit: through Jesus Christ our Lord. *Amen.*

O God, the Father of all, by whose guidance men plan wisely and do aright, we thank thee that it has been possible to open this place as a centre of happy fellowship for those who have to live in mean streets and overcrowded houses. Grant, we beseech thee, that here the *people* of this neighbourhood may enjoy friendship and freedom; we ask it in the name of him who came that men might have life, even Jesus Christ our Lord. *Amen.*

11. FOR THE PROFESSIONS

O God, who by thy Spirit in our hearts dost lead men to desire thy perfection, to seek for truth, and to rejoice in beauty; illumine and inspire, we beseech thee, all scientists, writers, artists, technicians, and craftsmen; that, in whatsoever is true and pure and lovely, thy Name may be

hallowed and thy Kingdom come on earth; through Jesus
Christ our Lord. *Amen.*

12. FOR HOME AND FAMILY LIFE

Heavenly Father, from whom all fatherhood in heaven
and earth is named; bless, we beseech thee, *these children*,
and give to *their* parents and to those in whose charge *they*
may be, the Spirit of wisdom and love; so that the home
in which *they* grow up may be to *them* an image of thy
Kingdom, and the care of *their* parents a likeness of thy
Love. *Amen.*

A Prayer for the Home. Looking Forward.

O Lord God, Giver of life and love, let thy blessing rest
upon us (those) whom thou hast drawn together in love.
Build thou our (their) home that it may be for all who live
in it a likeness of thy Kingdom. Give us (them) of thy
wisdom and patience that we (they) may walk together in
happiness and peace, be the way rough or smooth. If to us
(them) is given the joy of children and their care, grant us
(them) grace to bring them up in the knowledge of thee
and within the fellowship of thy holy Church; And in all
things and at all times be thou our Strength and our Guide;
through Jesus Christ our Lord. *Amen.*

A Thanksgiving. Looking Back.

O God, our heavenly Father, upon whose everlasting
arms the lives of thy children in this world are stayed; we
give thee heartfelt thanks for the joys and disciplines of our
homes in which we have known thy great love, and we
beseech thee continually to guide us to the perfect joy of
that eternal home, which thou hast prepared for them that
love thee, through thy dear Son, who shared our earthly

life and now reigns with thee in heaven, even Jesus Christ our Lord. *Amen.*

Almighty and all-loving Father, give us grace to be tender and thoughtful to those whom thou hast committed to our care. May we never as the years pass accept their presence and receive their service unnoticed. Give us understanding, self-control, and patience to make our home a happy place for those who live in it, and grant that those who come to it may be made more sure of thy love; for the sake of him who on the Cross took thought for his Mother's comfort and solace, even Jesus Christ our Lord. *Amen.*

13. A PRAYER FOR RELATIVES AND FRIENDS

Almighty God, whose goodness loved us into life and whose mercies never fail: we commend to thee those who are joined to us by the ties of kindred, friendship, and love; all children dear to us; all who help us to be faithful and whose goodness turns duties into love. Keep them both outwardly in their bodies and inwardly in their souls, and pour upon them the dew of thy blessing: through Jesus Christ our Lord. *Amen.*

14. FOR THOSE IN CAPTIVITY OR REFUGEES

Preserve, we pray thee, beloved Lord, in body and soul those who have been driven from home and country; and shorten the days till justice, peace, and goodwill are firmly established, and refugees may be reunited in their homes, for thy Name's sake. *Amen.*

15. FOR STRANGERS AND IMMIGRANTS

O God, the Father of all men, who hast bidden thy people to show kindness to the stranger; we pray for those who come from other countries to seek for work and make their homes in this land; help them and us to overcome the difficulties of custom, language, and race; surround them with companions who welcome and befriend them; and bless the societies which foster understanding and good-will; that in thy great family we may live as members one of another; through Jesus Christ our Lord. *Amen.*

16. FOR PEACE AT HOME AND IN THE WORLD

Grant, Lord, we beseech thee, that the course of this world may be so ordered in obedience to thy will that the people may live in security and freedom from want, and their children grow up to be makers of peace; for thy Name's sake. *Amen.*

We beseech thee, O Lord, to set the peace of heaven within the hearts of men that it may bind the nations also in a covenant which cannot be broken; through Jesus Christ our Lord. *Amen.*

17. FOR AN INDUSTRIAL AREA

O God, who dost love the children of men, we commend to thy care those who dwell in the towns in . . ., asking that they may live as befits thy children, and that loving thee they may love one another. Grant that in their lives they may witness to thee. Guide them in their citizenship by thy Holy Spirit, that their towns may become fair to behold, healthy to inhabit, and be filled with happy, and good homes. Grant to all who are engaged in industry a sense that they are engaged in thy work.

We commend to thy care those who are sick, unemployed, or otherwise distressed, praying that since thou dost care for them we also may be quick to help them.

Forgive the blindness and the selfishness which have

so often thwarted thy purpose; grant true repentance for sins of commission and for sins of omission: and give to us new vision and grace to do thy will; through Jesus Christ our Lord. *Amen.*

18. FOR INDUSTRY AND COMMERCE

O God, the Father of all, inspire us with such love, truth, and equity, that in our dealings one with another we may show forth our brotherhood in thee, for the sake of thy Son, our Lord Jesus Christ. *Amen.*

O God, the King of righteousness, lead us, we pray thee, in the ways of justice and of peace: inspire us to break down all oppression and wrong, to gain for every man his due reward, and from every man his due service; that each may live for all, and all may care for each; in the Name of Jesus Christ our Lord. *Amen.*

Almighty God who didst ordain that thy Son, Jesus Christ, should work with his hands to supply his own needs and the needs of others; teach us, we pray thee, that no labour is mean, and all labour is divine to which thou dost call us: through the same Jesus Christ our Lord. *Amen.*

O God, who providest for the creaturely needs of men and hast given them in Jesus Christ the food of their souls; forgive the stupidity and sin whereby men have abused thy providence and squandered thy gifts: Guide with thy just and peaceable wisdom those who take counsel for the nations and direct our industries; Grant that the day may quickly come when men shall be saved from too great anxiety for their daily bread, and from too great love of money and power. Inspire each of us to share more fairly the produce of thy world and be generous to feed the hungry and succour those in want; through Jesus Christ our Lord. *Amen.*

19. FOR AGRICULTURE

Give, O Lord, to all who till the ground the wisdom to understand thy laws, and to co-operate with thy wise ordering of the world. Give to men of science the power to discover the secrets of nature. Give to our statesmen the will to make just laws. Give to farmers and labourers the desire to work together in the spirit of justice and goodwill. And grant that the fruits of thy bountiful earth may not be hoarded by selfish men or squandered by foolish men, but that all who work may share abundantly in the harvest of thy soil, according to thy will, revealed to us in Jesus Christ our Lord. *Amen.*

20. FOR ALL WORKERS

Intercession

O God, the strength of them that labour and the rest of the weary; grant us when we are tired with our work to be recreated by thy Spirit; that being renewed for the service of thy Kingdom, we may serve thee gladly in freshness of body and mind; through Jesus Christ our Lord. *Amen.*

O God, who hast made the heaven and the earth and all that is good and lovely therein, and hast shown us through Jesus, our Lord, that the secret of joy is a heart freed from selfish desire; help us to find delight in simple things and ever to rejoice in the richness of thy bounty; through the same Jesus Christ our Lord. *Amen.*

Thanksgiving

Father of all, from whom comes every good and perfect gift; we thank thee for the joy we have in our homes, for the comradeship of fellow-workers, for the patience and courage of those who have fought for human rights and good conditions of life and work; for the continuing service of Trade Unions, Guilds, and Societies to

which we and our families belong. In praising thee for the
service of others and thy mercy given through them we
humbly offer thee the service of our own lives; through
Jesus Christ our Redeemer and Lord. *Amen.*

(B) THE SUFFRAGES OF THE LITANY ARRANGED AS INTERCESSIONS

*Because the Litany as a whole is felt nowadays to be too long
as an alternative to the State Prayers, etc., in Morning and
Evening Prayer and because in its existing form it is not easy
to abbreviate, it is used infrequently and is unfamiliar to many
of the laity. If the suffrages are re-grouped under the headings
the Church and the Nation, with one or two additions, they
say better than most modern litanies what we wish to ask.
The opening supplication can be used before either part;
similarly, as a conclusion, the section from* Son of God, we
beseech thee to hear us, *up to the Kyrie and then the final
collect. The opening and the closing supplications, together,
also make an Act of Devotion without the Intercessions.*

*In the third section we have made bold to add, in the light
of the poignant experience of refugee orphans in the world
today, the words* and motherless *after* fatherless.

I. OPENING SUPPLICATIONS

O God the Father, Creator of heaven and earth;
    have mercy upon us.
O God the Son, Redeemer of the world;
    have mercy upon us.
O God the Holy Spirit, proceeding from the Father
    and the Son;
    have mercy upon us.
O holy, blessed and glorious Trinity, three Persons
    and One God;
    have mercy upon us.

Remember not, Lord, our offences, nor the offences of our forefathers; neither take thou vengeance of our sins: spare us, good Lord, spare thy people, whom thou hast redeemed with thy most precious blood, and be not angry with us for ever,

Spare us, good Lord.

From all evil and mischief; from sin, from the crafts and assaults of the devil; from thy wrath, and from everlasting damnation,

Good Lord, deliver us.

From all blindness of heart; from pride, vainglory and hypocrisy; from envy, hatred, and malice, and all uncharitableness,

Good Lord, deliver us.

From fornication, and all other deadly sin; and from all the deceits of the world, the flesh, and the devil,

Good Lord, deliver us.

From lightning and tempest; from plague, pestilence, and famine; from battle and murder, and from sudden death,

Good Lord, deliver us.

From all sedition, privy conspiracy, and rebellion; from hardness of heart, and contempt of thy word and commandment,

Good Lord, deliver us.

By the mystery of thy holy Incarnation; by thy holy Nativity and Circumcision; by thy Baptism, Fasting, and Temptation,

Good Lord, deliver us.

By thine Agony and bloody Sweat; by thy Cross and Passion; by thy precious Death and Burial; by thy glorious

Resurrection and Ascension; and by the coming of the Holy Ghost,
Good Lord, deliver us.

In all time of our tribulation; in all time of our wealth; in the hour of death, and in the day of judgement,
Good Lord, deliver us.

2. FOR THE LIFE OF THE CHURCH

We sinners do beseech thee to hear us, O Lord God; and that it may please thee to rule and govern thy holy Church universal in the right way;
We beseech thee to hear us, good Lord.

That it may please thee to keep and strengthen in the true worshipping of thee, in righteousness and holiness of life, thy servant Elizabeth, our most gracious Queen and Governor;*
We beseech thee to hear us, good Lord.

That it may please thee to give us an heart to love and dread thee, and diligently to live after thy commandments;
We beseech thee to hear us, good Lord.

That it may please thee to illuminate all Bishops, Priests, and Deacons, with true knowledge and understanding of thy Word; and that both by their preaching and living they may set it forth and show it accordingly;
We beseech thee to hear us, good Lord.

[That it may please thee to bless thy servants at this time (to be) admitted to the Order of Deacons or of Priests, and to pour thy grace upon them; that they may duly execute their office to the edifying of thy Church, and to the glory of thy holy name;
We beseech thee to hear us, good Lord.]

* In countries outside the British Commonwealth the customary reference to the Head of State, e.g. the President of . . ., will be used.

That it may please thee to inspire continually the universal Church with the spirit of truth, unity, and concord; that all who confess thy holy name may agree in the truth of thy holy Word, and live in unity, and godly love;

We beseech thee to hear us, good Lord.

That it may please thee to further the work of thy Church in all the world, and to send forth labourers into the harvest;

We beseech thee to hear us, good Lord.

That it may please thee to bless and keep all thy people;

We beseech thee to hear us, good Lord.

That it may please thee to give us a heart to love and dread thee, and diligently to live after thy commandments;

We beseech thee to hear us, good Lord.

That it may please thee to give to all thy people increase of grace to hear meekly thy Word, and to receive it with pure affection, and to bring forth the fruits of the Spirit;

We beseech thee to hear us, good Lord.

That it may please thee to bring into the way of truth all such as have erred, and are deceived;

We beseech thee to hear us, good Lord.

That it may please thee to strengthen such as do stand; and to comfort and help the weak-hearted; and to raise up them that fall; and finally to beat down Satan under our feet;

We beseech thee to hear us, good Lord.

That it may please thee to succour, help, and comfort, all that are in danger, necessity, and tribulation.

We beseech thee to hear us, good Lord.

That it may please thee to forgive our enemies, persecutors, and slanderers, and to turn their hearts;
We beseech thee to hear us, good Lord.

That it may please thee to give us true repentance; to forgive us all our sins, negligences, and ignorances; and to endue us with the grace of thy Holy Spirit to amend our lives according to thy holy Word;
We beseech thee to hear us, good Lord.

. . .

Son of God: we beseech thee to hear us.
Son of God: we beseech thee to hear us.

O Lamb of God: that takest away the sins of the world;
Grant us thy peace.

O Lamb of God: that takest away the sins of the world;
Have mercy upon us.

O Christ, hear us.

Lord, have mercy upon us.
Christ, have mercy upon us.
Lord, have mercy upon us.

Let us say together:

We humbly beseech thee, O Father, mercifully to look upon our infirmities; and for the glory of thy Name turn from us all those evils that we most righteously have deserved; and grant, that in all our troubles we may put our whole trust and confidence in thy mercy, and evermore serve thee in holiness and pureness of living, to thy honour and glory; through our only Mediator and Advocate, Jesus Christ our Lord. Amen.

3. FOR THE LIFE OF THE NATION AND THE WORLD

We sinners do beseech thee to hear us, O Lord God;

and that it may please thee to rule and govern thy holy Church universal in the right way;
We beseech thee to hear us, good Lord.

That it may please thee to keep and strengthen in the true worshipping of thee, in righteousness and holiness of life, thy servant Elizabeth, our most gracious Queen and Governor;*
We beseech thee to hear us, good Lord.

That it may please thee to rule her heart in thy faith, fear, and love, and that she may evermore have affiance in thee, and ever seek thy honour and glory:
We beseech thee to hear us, good Lord.

That it may please thee to be her defender and keeper, giving her the victory over all her enemies;
We beseech thee to hear us, good Lord.

That it may please thee to bless and preserve Elizabeth the Queen Mother, Philip, Duke of Edinburgh, Charles, Prince of Wales, and all the Royal Family;
We beseech thee to hear us, good Lord.

That it may please thee to endue the High Court of Parliament, and all the Ministers of the Crown†, with grace, wisdom, and understanding;
We beseech thee to hear us, good Lord.

That it may please thee to bless and keep the Judges and‡ Magistrates, giving them grace to execute justice, and to maintain truth;
We beseech thee to hear us, good Lord.

* See footnote above (p. 189). The suffrages following, for the Royal Family, and for Parliament, would also be omitted.
† 'in our Commonwealth' may be added.
‡ As in the New Canadian Prayer Book.

That it may please thee to bless and prosper the forces of the Queen by sea, land, and air, and to shield them in all dangers and adversities;
   We beseech thee to hear us, good Lord.

That it may please thee to give to all nations unity, peace, and concord;
   We beseech thee to hear us, good Lord.

That it may please thee to succour, help, and comfort all that are in danger, necessity, and tribulation;
   We beseech thee to hear us, good Lord.

That it may please thee to preserve all that travel, all women labouring of child, all sick persons, and young children; and to shew thy pity upon all prisoners and captives;
   We beseech thee to hear us, good Lord.

That it may please thee to bless our homes and families, that those who marry may live together according to the laws and children may grow up in thy fear and love;
   We beseech thee to hear us, good Lord.

That it may please thee to defend, and provide for, the fatherless and motherless children, and widows, and all that are desolate and oppressed;
   We beseech thee to hear us, good Lord.

That it may please thee to give and preserve to our use the kindly fruits of the earth, so as in due time we may enjoy them;
   We beseech thee to hear us, good Lord.

That it may please thee to prosper the industries of our land, and that men may deal justly with one another and serve the common good;
   We beseech thee to hear us, good Lord.

That it may please thee to have mercy upon all men;
We beseech thee to hear us, good Lord.

That it may please thee to give us true repentance; to forgive us all our sins, negligences, and ignorances; and to endue us with the grace of thy Holy Spirit to amend our lives according to thy Holy Word;
We beseech thee to hear us, good Lord.

. . .

Son of God: we beseech thee to hear us.
Son of God: we beseech thee to hear us.

O Lamb of God: that takest away the sins of the world;
Grant us thy peace.

O Lamb of God: that takest away the sins of the world;
Have mercy upon us.

O Christ, hear us.

Lord, have mercy upon us.
Christ, have mercy upon us.
Lord, have mercy upon us.

Let us say together.

We humbly beseech thee, O Father, mercifully to look upon our infirmities; and for the glory of thy name turn from us all those evils that we most righteously have deserved; and grant, that in all our troubles we may put our whole trust and confidence in thy mercy, and evermore serve thee in holiness and pureness of living, to thy honour and glory; through our only Mediator and Advocate, Jesus Christ our Lord. Amen.

EDITORIAL NOTE AND
A DEDICATION

It is forty-three years since the Oxford Diocesan Service Book was issued and thirty-two years since that of Southwark was published. Both have been a stand-by to bishops and clergy, but they are out of print, and rather dated. Therefore one hopes that, for a time, this book may be of some practical service to bishops and clergy. It is also published in the hope that it may help to lift public worship out of the rut into which it falls. Public worship too often neither reaches the heights nor makes contact with the life and work of contemporary society. Experience has shown that care with the ordering of services for special occasions tends to increase the care taken over the regular services. These occasional services may even open men's eyes to see what worship may be in their lives and to stimulate a hunger that a dull and lifeless performance of the statutory services cannot satisfy.

A priest and congregation who try to make the Sunday services an offering to God for him to bless and use are serving the mission of the Church in society well. It was a true instinct of primitive man which made him set his altars on the high hills. If our theology is soundly Christian there is no conflict between the uplift of prayer and adoration and the outreach of Christian action in the service of men. Since God is Love, they are not alternatives but complementary; and the one is impoverished without the other.

Much in this book follows traditional uses. Its prayers are from many sources, ancient and modern. Among the latter I have drawn upon two books by Dr. Milner-White, the late Dean of York, *A Cambridge Bede Book* (Longmans, Green and Co.), and *A Procession of Passion Prayers*, printed privately for the author and then published for him by the S.P.C.K. My debt to him in liturgical matters is much greater than these borrowings. I have also drawn on compilations in which I had some share, *A Students' Book of Prayers* (S.C.M. Press), *The Kingdom, the Power, and the Glory* (O.U.P.), *New Every Morning* (B.B.C.). To other contemporaries whose authorship I have not been able to trace, my thanks are also due. Every prayer made and offered to God is a free gift in the service of God. Therefore anyone is free to use what they wish from this book, so far as my copyright is concerned.*

I have also to thank those who in past years co-operated in the preparation of some of the orders of service in it, and also those who recently have advised and helped in preparing the book for publication, particularly the Revs. Gordon Hewitt and Raymond Hockley and the Ven. Peter Bostock.

I would dedicate it to the memory of my father, who cared for these things.

✠ L.S.H.

August 1964.

---

* Details of these and other sources of copyright material will be found on the following page.

ACKNOWLEDGEMENTS

Thanks are due to the following copyright holders for permission to use material under their control, as follows:

Mrs. L. A. Anson, for the prayer 'Give, O Lord, to all who till the ground', by the Rev. Harold Anson (p. 186); Messrs. Jonathan Cape Ltd., for the prayer 'Jesus, Master, Carpenter' from *The Road*, by Harry Martinson (p. 160); Miss D. E. Collins and Messrs. A. P. Watt & Son, for the carol 'How far is it to Bethlehem' (pp. 149–50); The Custodian of the *Book of Common Prayer of the Protestant Episcopal Church of the U.S.A.*, for the prayer 'Almighty God, whose most dear Son went not up to joy' (pp. 60, 159); The Rev. H. F. Leatherland, for the prayer 'O God, the Father of all men' (p. 183); Longmans, Green & Co. Ltd., for four prayers from *A Cambridge Bede Book*, compiled by Eric Milner-White (pp. 31, 48 and 94, 61, 184); Mrs. S. C. Mess, for the prayer 'O God, who dost ever love' (p. 184); A. R. Mowbray & Co. Ltd., for the translations of 'Unto us is born a Son' (p. 146) and 'In dulci jubilo' (p. 148) from *The Cowley Carol Book*, and for the prayer 'O God and Father of all' (p. 14) from *After The Third Collect*, compiled by Eric Milner-White; the Publications Committee of the Episcopal Church of Scotland for the prayer 'O Lord God, our heavenly Father, regard, we beseech thee, with thy divine pity', adapted from *The Scottish Prayer Book* (p. 160); S.P.C.K., for three prayers from *A Procession of Passion Prayers*, compiled by Eric Milner-White (pp. 158, 161, 163), and for the prayer in commemoration of St. Hugh of Lincoln (p. 177) from *Black Letter Saints' Days*, compiled by Bishop W. H. Frere, D.D.; Mrs. William Temple, for the prayer 'O God, the King of righteousness', by Archbishop Temple (p. 185).

The copyright of the hymns 'Judge eternal, throned in splendour' (from *The English Hymnal*) and 'Fairest Lord Jesus' is controlled by Oxford University Press. The prayers *For Healing, For a Sick Child, For a Dying Child, For a Convalescent* and *For One Troubled in Conscience* (pp. 108–110), and 'Almighty God, Father of all mercies' (p. 116) are reprinted from *The Prayer Book as Proposed in 1928* by permission of the holders of the copyright. The material from The Authorized Version of the Bible and *The Book of Common Prayer* is Crown Copyright and is reprinted by permission.

The prayer 'O God who hast called us' (p. 179), by the late Bishop C. M. Blagden, was included in his Booklet of Occasional Prayers, compiled for the Diocese of Peterborough. The prayers 'O God, before whose face' (p. 15) and 'Almighty God, whose goodness' (p. 183) are slightly adapted from *Devotional Services* (J. M. Dent Ltd.), compiled by the late Dr. John Hunter, and those beginning 'O Lord God, our Creator' (p. 31), 'O God, who hast made this holy night' (p. 145), 'O God, who hast taught us' (p. 180), 'O God, who by thy Spirit' (p. 181), 'O God, the Father of all' (p. 185), and 'O God, who hast made the heaven and the earth' (p. 186) are from *The Grey Book*.

FIRST LINES OF HYMNS, WITH RECOMMENDED TUNES

Key to Abbreviations: EH = *The English Hymnal*; EHSB = *The English Hymnal Service Book*; AM = *Hymns Ancient and Modern*; AMR = *Hymns Ancient and Modern Revised*; SP = *Songs of Praise*; BBC = *The BBC Hymn Book*; OBC = *The Oxford Book of Carols*; CCB = *The Cowley Carol Book*.

A number printed in brackets and italics indicates a suggested alternative tune.
An asterisk against a page number indicates that the first line only of the hymn appears in the book.

Page No.	First Line	Some sources and suggested tunes	Author, Translator, etc.
154*	All glory, laud, and honour	EH 622, EHSB 5, AMR 98, SP 135	*Latin*, St. Theodulph of Orleans, d. 821. *Tr.* J. M. Neale, 1818–66
1, 16*, 131	All people that on earth do dwell	EH 365, EHSB 7, AMR 166, SP 443	W. Kethe, Daye's Psalter, 1560–1
16*	All things are thine: no gift have we	EH 173, SP 189	J. G. Whittier, 1807–92
57*, 58	Alleluya, King eternal (*final verse of* Alleluya, sing to Jesus)	EH 301, EHSB 11, AMR 399, SP 260	W. Chatterton Dix, 1837–98
150*	Angels, from the realms of glory	EHSB 320, SP 71	J. Montgomery, 1771–1854
151*	As with gladness men of old	EH 39, EHSB 17, AMR 79, SP 83	W. Chatterton Dix, 1837–98
99*	Breathe on me, Breath of God	SP 458, (*EHSB 274*), (*AMR 362*)	Edwin Hatch, 1835–89
70	Christ be with me, Christ within me (*verse 8 of* I bind unto myself today)	EH 212 ii, EHSB 102 ii	*Ascribed to* St. Patrick, 372–466. *Tr.* Mrs. C. F. Alexander, 1818–95

Page No.	First Line	Some sources and suggested tunes	Author, Translator, etc.
14,*, 16*, 99*	Christ is our corner-stone	EHSB 301, AMR 243	J. Chandler, 1806–76, *based on* Angularis fundamentum
99*	City of God, how broad and far	EH 375, EHSB 41, AMR 258, SP 468	S. Johnson, 1822–82
99*	Come down, O Love divine	EH 152, EHSB 43, SP 177	Bianco da Siena, d. 1434. *Tr.* R. F. Littledale, 1833–90
23*, 32*, 37*, 46*	Come, Holy Ghost, our souls inspire	EHSB 44, AMR 157, SP 178, (*EH 154*)	Bishop J. Cosin, 1594–1672, *based on* Veni, Creator Spiritus
142, 149*	Fairest Lord Jesus	BBC 138, 139	*Anon.*, Münster, 1677. *Tr.* Lilian Sinclair Stevenson, 1870–1960
100*	Father, hear the prayer we offer	EH 385, EHSB 60, SP 487	Mrs. L. M. Willis, 1824–1908
100*	Fill thou my life, O Lord my God	EHSB 304, AMR 373, SP 492	Horatius Bonar, 1808–89
133*, 140*	For all the Saints who from their labours rest	EH 641, EHSB 66, SP 202	Bishop William Walsham How, 1823–97
121	Give rest, O Christ, to thy servant	EH 744	Russian Contakion of the Departed. *Tr.* W. J. Birkbeck, 1859–1916
99*	Glorious things of thee are spoken	EH 393, EHSB 74, AMR 257 ii, SP 500	John Newton, 1725–1807
16*, 33*, 119*	Happy are they, they that love God	EH 398, EHSB 86, AMR 261, SP 509	C. Coffin, 1676–1749. *Tr.* Robert Bridges, 1844–1930

Page No.	First Line	Some sources and suggested tunes	Author, Translator, etc.
149*	Hark! the herald Angels sing	EH 24, EHSB 90, AMR 60, SP 74	Charles Wesley, 1707–88, G. Whitefield, 1714–70, M. Madan, 1726–90, and others
71*, 100*	He who would valiant be	EH 402, EHSB 94, SP 515	Percy Dearmer, 1867–1936, after John Bunyan, 1628–88
133*	Help us to help each other, Lord	BBC 378, SP 517	Charles Wesley, 1707–88, alt.
149	How far is it to Bethlehem	OBC 142	Frances Chesterton, 1870–1938
68, 70, 95	I bind unto myself today	EH 212 i, EHSB 102 i, SP 528	Ascribed to St. Patrick, 372–466. Tr. Mrs. C. F. Alexander, 1818–95
21*	Immortal, invisible	EH 407, EHSB 103, AMR 372, SP 535	W. Chalmers Smith, 1824–1908
148	In dulci jubilo	CCB 12	German, 14th century. Tr. G. R. Woodward, 1848–1934
143, 149*	In the bleak mid-winter	EH 25, EHSB 107, AMR 67, SP 75	Christina Georgina Rossetti, 1830–94
157	It is a thing most wonderful	EH 597, SP 602, BBC 81	Bishop William Walsham How, 1823–97
100*, 141*	Jesus, good above all other	EH 598, EHSB 119, BBC 72, SP 540	Percy Dearmer, 1867–1936
100*, 133*, 139*	Jesus shall reign where'er the sun	EH 420, EHSB 121, AMR 220, SP 545 (with alleluyas, EH 519, EHSB 297, AMR 172)	Isaac Watts, 1674–1748

Page No.	First Line	Some sources and suggested tunes	Author, Translator, etc.
16*	Jesus, where'er thy people meet	EH 422, EHSB 123, AMR 245	William Cowper, 1731–1800
40	Judge eternal, throned in splendour	EH 423, EHSB 124, BBC 393, SP 552	Henry Scott Holland, 1847–1918
99*	Lift up your heads, ye gates of brass	EH 549, (166), SP 301	J. Montgomery, 1771–1854
151	Lully, lulla, thou little tiny child	OBC 22	Coventry Carol, 15th century, from the Pageant of the Shearmen and Tailors
16*	Now thank we all our God	EH 533, EHSB 159, AMR 379, SP 350	M. Rinkart, 1586–1649. Tr. Catherine Winkworth, 1827–78
147*	O come, all ye faithful	EH 28, EHSB 164, AMR 59, SP 78	Latin, J. Wade, c. 1711–86. Tr. F. Oakley, 1802–80, W. T. Brooke, 1848–1916, and others
131	O enter then his gates with praise (3rd and 4th verses of All people that on earth do dwell)	EH 365, EHSB 7, AMR 166, SP 443	W. Kethe, Daye's Psalter, 1560–1
6	O friends, in gladness let us sing (final verse of Ye watchers and ye holy ones)	EH 519, EHSB 297	Athelstan Riley, 1858–1945
119*	O God of Bethel, by whose hand	EH 447, (43), EHSB 174, (130), AMR 299	P. Doddridge, 1702–51, and Michael Bruce, 1746–67

Page No.	First Line	Some sources and suggested tunes	Author, Translator, etc.
44, 100*	O God of truth, whose living word	EH 449, AMR 309, SP 597	T. Hughes, 1823–96
126, 155*	O Jesu, king most wonderful	EH 419, Part II (EHSB 99), AMR 189, Part II, (AMR 69)	Latin, 11th century. Tr. Edward Caswall, 1814–78
147*	O little town of Bethlehem	EH 15, EHSB 181, AMR 65, SP 79	Bishop Phillips Brooks, 1835–93
157*	O sacred head, sore wounded	EH 102, EHSB 186, SP 128	P. Gerhardt, 1607–76, based on Salve caput cruentatum (ascribed to St. Bernard). Tr. Robert Bridges, 1844–1930
99*	O thou who camest from above	EH 343, (167), EHSB 190, AMR 329, (268)	Charles Wesley, 1707–88
13, 130, 136	Praise God, from whom all blessings flow (Doxology)	EH 267, (365), EHSB 76, (7), AMR 23, (166), SP 413	Bishop Thomas Ken, 1637–1711
133*	Praise, my soul, the King of heaven	EH 470, EHSB 206, AMR 365, SP 623	H. F. Lyte, 1793–1847
16*, 133*, 138*	Praise to the Lord, the Almighty, the King of creation	EH 536, EHSB 209, AMR 382, SP 626	J. Neander, 1650–80. Tr. Catherine Winkworth, 1827–78, and (in EH) Percy Dearmer, 1867–1936
4, 39*, 140*	Pray that Jerusalem may have	EH 472, EHSB 210, SP 628	Scottish Psalter, 1650
100*	Strong Captain, in thy holy ranks	AMR 461	J. M. C. Crum, 1872–1958

Page No.	First Line	Some sources and suggested tunes	Author, Translator, etc.
156*	Ride on, ride on in majesty	EH 620, EHSB 213, SP 137, (AMR 2)	H. H. Milman, 1791–1868
16*, 24*, 60*, 135*	The Church of God a kingdom is	(EH 93), (EHSB 243), AMR 254	L. B. C. L. Muirhead, 1845–1925
119*	The God of love my Shepherd is	EH 93, EHSB 243, AMR 178, SP 653	George Herbert, 1593–1633
119*	The Lord's my Shepherd, I'll not want	EHSB 313, (99), (AMR 69)	Scottish Psalter, 1650
121*	This joyful Eastertide	CCB 51, (OBC 152)	G. R. Woodward, 1848–1934
68*	Thou whose almighty word	EH 553, EHSB 266, AM 360, AMR 266, (SP 303)	J. Marriott, 1780–1825
124	Thy hand, O God, has guided	EH 545, EHSB 271, AMR 256	E. H. Plumptre, 1821–91
100*	Thy kingdom come! on bended knee	EH 504, EHSB 272, AMR 263, SP 680	F. L. Hosmer, 1840–1929
146	Unto us is born a Son	CCB 25 (to different translation, SP 385, OBC 12)	15th century, from Piae Cantiones. Tr. G. R. Woodward, 1848–1934
138	Worship, honour, glory, blessing (Part II of Praise the Lord, ye heavens, adore him)	(EH 393), EHSB 207, AMR 368, SP 418	E. Osler, 1798–1863
133*	Ye holy Angels bright	EH 517, EHSB 295, AMR 371, SP 701	R. Baxter, 1615–91, and J. H. Gurney, 1802–62
16*, 71*, 100*, 128, 141*	Ye servants of God, your Master proclaim	AMR 226	Charles Wesley, 1707–88